Simplicity
How to use a
SEWING MACHINE

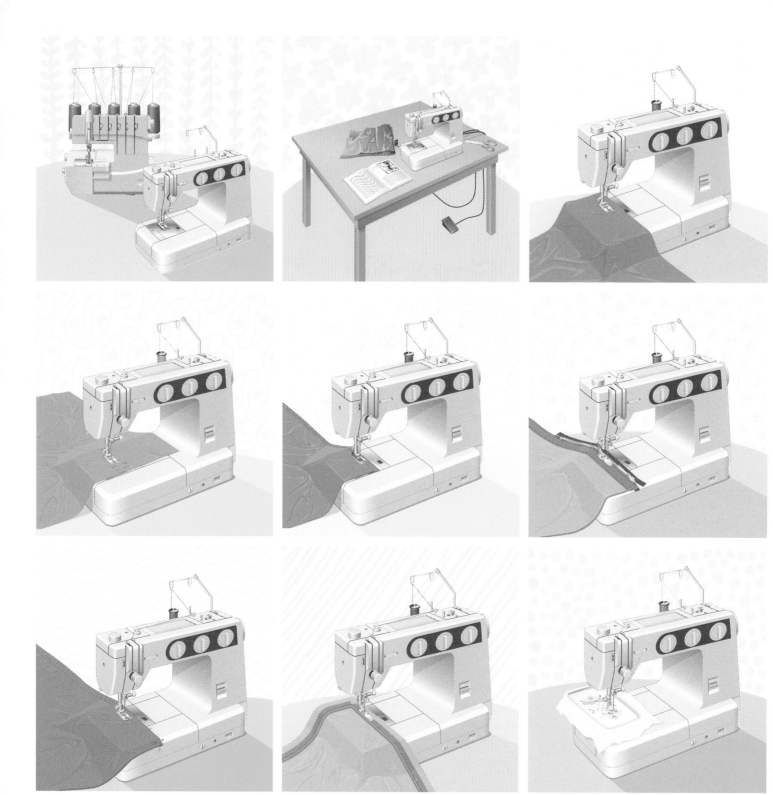

Simplicity®
How to use a
SEWING MACHINE
Everything you need to know to sew with confidence

Marie Clayton

COLLINS & BROWN

SIMPLICITY
HOW TO USE A SEWING MACHINE

First published in the United Kingdom
in 2010 by
Collins & Brown
10 Southcombe Street
London, W14 0RA

An imprint of Anova Books Company Ltd

ISBN 978-1-84340-554-2

A CIP catalogue for this book is available
from the British Library.

10 9 8 7 6 5 4 3 2 1

Reproduction by Mission, Hong Kong
Printed and bound by 1010 Printing
International Ltd, China

This book can be ordered direct from
the publisher at **www.anovabooks.com**

AUTHOR ACKNOWLEDGMENTS

With thanks to everyone at Collins & Brown for their
support of this book, particularly Katie Cowan, Miriam
Hyslop and Nina Sharman. Thank you to Kuo Kang
Chen for the excellent illustrations, Cheryl Brown for
her thorough editing and Smith & Gilmour for the
stylish design. I would also like to thank Deborah
Shepherd, Ron Stower and Maureen Brown at Janome,
Stephen Bogod at Singer and Dawn Cowling at Bernina
for all their help with technical information and for
answering endless questions.

Marie Clayton

CONTENTS

BEFORE YOU BEGIN

Sewing is a practical skill that is useful for running repairs and it can also be a great outlet for your creativity. There are so many interesting fabrics available today, as well as wonderful buttons and trims, that you can make something unique and personal with just a little time and effort.

THE BOOK FOR YOU

Modern sewing machines and sergers have so many exciting features that they can look a bit daunting to a less experienced sewer – but these not only make repetitive or complex tasks quick and stress-free, they can also open up a new world of decorative techniques.

This book is designed to help you to choose the right machine for you, and then explains how to get the very best from it whatever you want to make.

BUYING THE RIGHT MACHINE

Chapter 1, Choosing a Machine, covers the different machines available, from a simple manual right through to the multifunction computerized models. There is advice on what particular features to look out for, depending on the type of sewing you want to do, complete with a handy flow chart to help you make your choice. Chapter 2, Knowing Your Machine, begins with how to set up your sewing area for efficient working, and then goes into a guided tour of a typical sewing machine and serger, with details of the main working parts and what they do. It covers the different types of presser foot and needle for the sewing machine and what they are used for. There are illustrated steps for basic techniques such as how to wind a bobbin on your sewing machine, and how to thread up for both the sewing machine and the serger, including how to set the correct tension on the threads for perfect stitch formation.

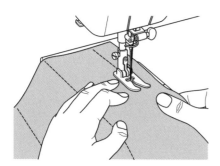

◀ Chapter 3, Using Your Machine, will give you the confidence to get started with your new sewing machine.

GETTING STARTED

In Chapter 3, Using Your Machine, we get started on sewing, with explanations of how to set up your machine and how to stitch and guide the fabric. A useful stitch glossary covers the basic stitches that are commonly available on the sewing machine and the serger. Troubleshooting sections look at common stitching or operational problems, what might have caused them, and how to put them right. A brief section on fabric covers the different types, and explains how best to handle some special fabrics. The chapter ends with information on other sewing equipment you will need for measuring, marking and cutting, along with a step-by-step basic skills section covering pinning, basting and simple hand-stitching techniques.

▼ Chapter 1, Choosing a Machine, will help you to choose the right machine for your needs.

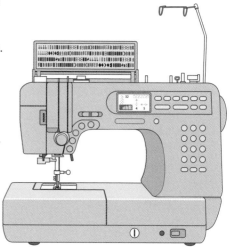

SEWING TECHNIQUES

The remainder of the book introduces sewing techniques that you can use your machine for. Chapter 4, Sewing Seams, covers the most often used types of seam, with illustrated steps explaining how to stitch each one. There is also a short section with a range of techniques to finish the raw edges of the seam allowance after stitching a straight-forward seam, to give a more professional look to your sewing. In addition this chapter covers how to handle corners and curves, as well as stitching darts. Chapter 5, Sewing Hems, covers both basic techniques and decorative treatments, while Chapter 6, Zippers and Buttonholes, looks at the different ways of inserting zippers and adding buttons, buttonholes and other closures. In Chapter 7, Gathers, Tucks and Pleats, we start on some decorative techniques, with how to handle gathers, tucks and pleats for a perfect result every

time. Chapter 8, Binding and Trimming, details the best techniques for making and adding binding or piping, as well as sewing on store-bought trims. Chapter 9, Decorative Techniques, is all about embellishing techniques, such as machine embroidery, appliqué, patchwork and quilting, including the basic steps for making a complete quilt. At the end of the book is an extensive glossary, which explains all the sewing terms used in the book for quick reference.

LEARNING BY DOING

One of the major benefits of being able to sew is that you are no longer tied to the colors and styles available in the stores – you can make whatever you like in whatever fabric you choose. And even if you don't have time to make a complete project from scratch, many of the techniques in this book can be used

to personalize store-bought items so they are one-of-a-kind. Learning to sew is the first step into an exciting new world; learning to make the most of your sewing machine will help you to build your skills quickly to achieve professional-looking results. Don't be afraid to experiment on your machine – you may find a wonderful new way to accomplish something and even the odd disaster can usually be turned into something different. One of the joys of fabric is that it is so forgiving – there aren't many types that cannot be unpicked and stitched again.

If you are new to sewing, start by making something quite simple and straightforward that will allow you to concentrate on learning to use your machine and understanding what the different functions will do for you. As you progress in confidence and skill you can move on to more complex projects – the only way to become an experienced sewer is by doing lots of sewing!

▼ Chapter 2, Knowing Your Machine, provides essential advice on choosing presser feet and sewing machine needles whatever the sewing task to be undertaken.

▼ Chapters 4 to 8 outline all the practical tasks you can use your sewing machine for including sewing seams, hemming and making trimmings.

▼ Chapter 9, Decorative Techniques, introduces some of the creative embellishments that your sewing machine can help you to achieve.

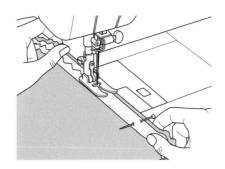
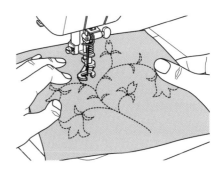

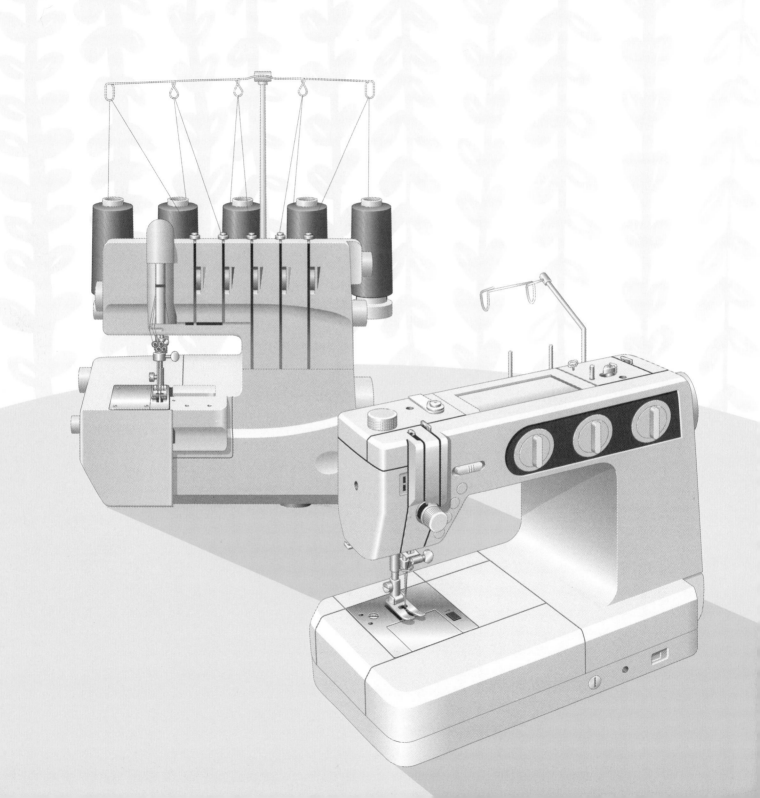

CHOOSING A MACHINE

Sewing is an exciting and rewarding pastime that will not only save you money but also allow you to make something that is uniquely yours. Today, it has never been easier to make your own professionally finished soft furnishings, clothes and accessories with a wide range of sewing machines on the market to help you. But how do you choose the right machine for your needs? This chapter will give you all the information you need to help you to decide which is the perfect sewing machine for you.

TYPES OF SEWING MACHINE

There are many different types of sewing machine available on the market, ranging from basic designs with only a small selection of stitches to computerized models that can automatically stitch detailed embroidery designs from a picture or photograph.

WHICH MACHINE?

While most sewing machines are suitable for a range of sewing jobs, some are designed for a specific task and will not be multipurpose. As a general rule, the more stitches and functions a machine has the more expensive it will be. However, there is very little point in paying extra for features you just won't use. Begin by taking an overview of the different types of sewing machine available to you.

MANUAL MACHINES

Manual sewing machines are operated by turning a hand wheel with one hand or by pumping on a treadle with your foot. Many old, reconditioned manual machines are still going strong and can be found on auction sites or in antique stores. Generally, such machines can only perform basic stitching, but for most straightforward sewing they are perfectly adequate, if a little slow. They are sturdy and simple to service – there is little to go wrong on them – and ideal if there is not a reliable electricity supply. Machines for children are usually manual and although these are really only toys they will stitch a basic seam. Manual machines for adults are still made, particularly for communities that do not use electricity, such as the Amish. These machines generally offer several different stitches, a buttonhole function and zigzag.

An antique manual sewing machine has little to go wrong and well-serviced or reconditioned machines may still work well.

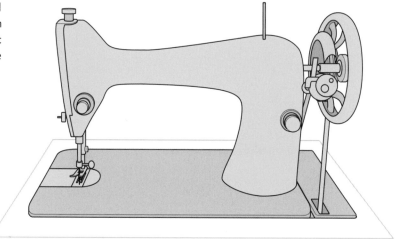

ELECTRIC MACHINES

An electric sewing machine has a motor in the body that moves the needle up and down, coordinating it with the movement of the feed dog and bobbin mechanism below the needle plate (see Fabric Feed, page 16, for more details). The motor is usually driven by a foot pedal – the harder you press your foot down the faster you sew, while the feed dog automatically feeds the fabric under the needle at the correct speed. The foot pedal allows you to keep both hands free to guide the fabric. The stitch type, width and length are selected by turning dials. There is a wide range of electric machines available, from inexpensive basic machines with only a few stitch options to more expensive models with lots of stitches to choose from.

THINGS TO CONSIDER

✂ Electric machines are much faster and more accurate than antique manual models.

✂ Once you have selected an electric machine you will not be able to add more stitches or functions later, so make sure it will do everything you may need for the foreseeable future.

✂ A second-hand electric machine will give you more built-in functions for your money, but you should make sure that it is a reputable brand in good working order.

✂ Some early electric machines had each stitch pattern on a small pattern disc (see page 18). If you buy a second-hand machine that operates this way, ensure it has a good selection of discs as you will find it difficult to source more.

✂ A cheap, no-brand supermarket buy may seem to have all the functions you need, but will it be sturdy enough for frequent use? Accessories may not be available to buy later, and you should check that you can adjust the stitch width and length, as if these are preset your stitching options will be limited.

▼ A budget electric machine has no fancy extras so it is very simple to operate. It will only have a small range of preset stitches and may not have some functions, such as the option to adjust the stitch width; however, it will be fine for basic sewing.

▼ A mid-range electric machine will have a wider range of preset stitches, including a one-step automatic buttonhole, the ability to adjust stitch width as well as length, and extra functions, such as adjustable foot pressure. Check which extra functions you need before making a final decision between different models.

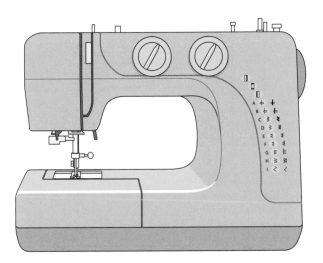

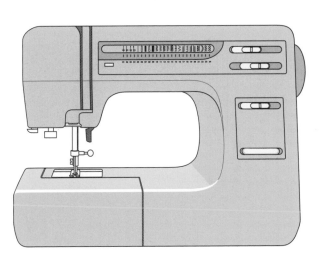

COMPUTERIZED MACHINES

Computerized sewing machines have many more stitches than ordinary electric machines and often include extra functions to allow you to create your own simple patterns. A computerized machine has several motors that power the different functions of the machine, giving precise control and making it possible to produce hundreds of different stitches. It contains computer chips with the correct tension, length and width for each stitch style programed in by the manufacturer, and in addition these can usually be adjusted to create special effects. Stitches are selected either by pressing a key or by using a touch pad linked to an LCD screen on the front of the machine. Many computerized machines feature the ability to memorize sequences of stitches so you can create and store designs you use often. On top-of-the-range models you may also be able to copy extra stitch patterns onto the machine from a CD or memory card, connect to the Internet via computer to download new designs, or use your computer to create personalized designs.

Using software

Customizing and digitizing software can be used in conjunction with computerized sewing machines but it will require a separate computer to run on. Before buying any software, do make sure your computer has the correct specification to run it. The subject of software is too complex to go into in detail here, but if this is an area you are interested in, look at the available software first and choose the best program for your needs, then check out the sewing machine models compatible with it. And remember, on some machines you can create and save stitch sequences and motifs – if this is all you require you may not need software.

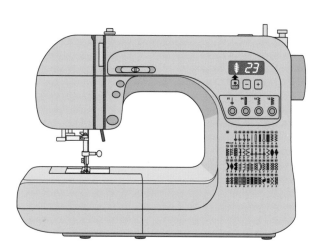

▼ A basic computerized machine will have a wide range of preset stitches, including several buttonhole designs, and stitch width and length can be used as preset or adjusted to create special effects.

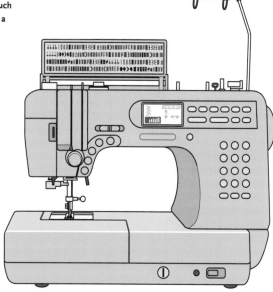

▶ A higher-specification computerized machine will have hundreds of preset stitches, as well as extra functions, such as the ability to create and memorize a stitch sequence.

EMBROIDERY MACHINE

These are designed mainly for embroidery, although some models have general sewing functions too. The entry-level machines generally stitch all the parts of the embroidery design that are in one color and then stop until the next color thread is threaded onto the machine. Some of the more expensive machines will switch automatically between several different color threads which are threaded up at the start. As well as offering a range of embroidery stitches, motifs and borders are also included, and new designs can often be purchased and added as required. It may also be possible to create your own designs using design software on a computer; and, with some models, designs can be edited on screen before they are stitched.

▼ A top-of-the-range multifunctional embroidery machine will offer extra functions, such as being able to plan out large stitch sequences and the ability to embroider or quilt across a large area in sections without a visible join.

THINGS TO CONSIDER

✂ If you want to stitch large motifs, check the maximum embroidery area the machine can handle.

✂ For embroidery with large blocks of color, a machine that can take cones of thread rather than spools will need rethreading less often.

✂ If the machine uses many colors simultaneously, an automatic threading feature will save time.

✂ Some models allow you to rotate, mirror and enlarge designs. Decide how much flexibility you need to alter the patterns provided.

✂ If you want to use computer design software, check it is compatible to the model you choose.

✂ If you are likely to stitch large areas of complex embroidery regularly, check the stitch speed – 650 stitches a minute is reasonably fast, 1,000 stitches a minute will save more time.

✂ A combination embroidery/sewing machine is more compact than having two separate machines, so, if space is an issue, it may be sensible to buy an embroidery machine that has general sewing functions too.

▶ If you are investing in a basic machine solely for embroidery, it will save you time to choose one that can be threaded with all the colors needed before you start and that changes between colors automatically.

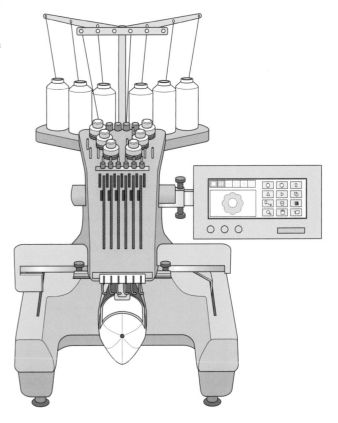

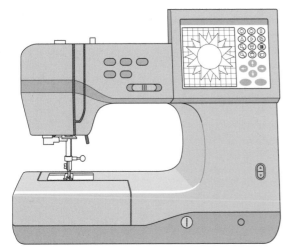

SERGER

A serger or overlock sewing machine can stitch a seam, trim, and finish the edge all in one step, giving a professional finish to garments and other projects. A serger is so much faster than a conventional sewing machine for such work, but it is unable to offer the full range of sewing functions, such as buttonholes and topstitching, for instance. However, if you are a regular sewer, the serger may be worth investing in for sewing hems and seams. Depending on the model you choose, it may also offer built-in functions or the possibility to purchase attachments for stitching rolled hems, gathering, attaching bindings, creating special effects and making decorative edgings.

A serger stitches in a different way than a conventional sewing machine. Stitches are formed by needle threads combining with looper threads which take the place of the bobbins. Sergers can stitch with two, three, four or five threads, using different combinations of needles and loopers. A machine with the capability to handle more threads can also be set up to use less, so will be more versatile. Cutting blades can be set to trim the fabric edge immediately in front of the stitching as it is formed. For more about how the serger works and different serger stitches, see pages 42–47 and 61–66.

THINGS TO CONSIDER

✂ Generally a serger will not replace a general sewing machine. However, it will save you the time that you would otherwise spend finishing off raw edges and is useful for creating special effects, so it is worth investing in if you plan to do a lot of sewing.

✂ With some of the less expensive sergers, the fabric may stretch and pucker as you stitch. This is quite a common problem, so be sure to try out several models before you buy.

✂ Some sergers use standard sewing machine needles, but many models use special needles, so make sure these are easy to purchase.

✂ For more sewing options, choose a machine with differential feed (see page 43). This will enable you, for example, to adjust the feed when working with knits to obtain a good flat seam, to speed up the feed to create a ruffle on a single layer of woven fabric, or to create a waved edge effect.

✂ There are now several lightweight inexpensive sergers on the market, but be very wary of these. A serger is designed to sew at quite a rate, so it needs some weight to keep it firm and steady on the table. A very light machine may start to jump around as you speed up, which can be dangerous.

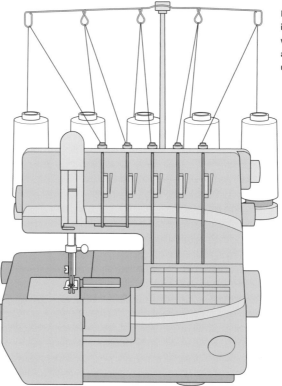

If you want a professional finish to the inside of your projects, a serger is just what you need. The high-end models are more versatile and can also be used for decorative effects.

SEWING MACHINE FEATURES

To help you to decide which sewing machine is the right one for you, it is useful to know how a sewing machine works, to have an understanding of the common features shared by most machines – and how these might differ from model to model – and to be aware of any special features offered.

A COMPACT UNIT

The workings of the domestic sewing machine are protected within a strong, molded body. Hinged sections provide access to some parts, such as the bobbin case or threading areas, stitch selectors or a built-in tool compartment. These will vary from model to model, but you should never open up any other part of the case or you may invalidate the manufacturer's warranty. The flat bed provides a surface for the fabric that is being stitched to rest on as it is fed between the upper and lower threading runs. On some sewing machine models the flat bed area can be extended or reduced according to the fabric area to be stitched.

Extension table

An extension table fits onto the machine at the needle end and gives a much larger sewing bed to support large pieces of sewing, such as quilts or drapes. When no longer needed, it can be removed again so the machine is easier to store away (see page 20).

Free arm

If a machine has a free-arm facility, it is usually brought into use by detaching a piece on the base of the machine, leaving the arm protruding. Narrow cylindrical items, such as sleeves and pant legs, can then be threaded onto the arm for easier stitching (see page 20).

> **TIP** Visit a specialist retailer for advice on buying a sewing machine and take the chance to try out as many different models as possible. Testing the machine's buttonhole function is a good way to check that it makes even, balanced stitches in all directions.

▼ This sewing machine has a hinged case on its top that opens to reveal the start of the upper threading run.

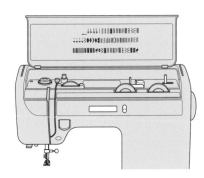

THE NEEDLE THREAD

The upper thread runs from the thread spool through thread guides, the tension mechanism and the take-up lever to the needle (for more detail on how to thread a machine, see page 38). Most machines thread more or less in the same way with only minor variations, so once you have learned the principles of threading you should be able to figure out how to thread almost any standard machine. However, it always helps to have a diagram and some modern machines have the threading run marked on the case in some way, which is useful for a beginner sewer.

Thread guides

Thread guides keep the thread in line as it goes from the spool to the needle. There are usually one or two between the spool and the tension mechanism, one on the front of the machine after the take-up lever, and one on either side of the needle. The thread guides can either be a small knob with disks to slide the thread between, a wire loop or an open-ended metal hook.

▼ For most home décor projects you can manage quite happily without a free arm, but if you intend to do a lot of dressmaking, it will be invaluable.

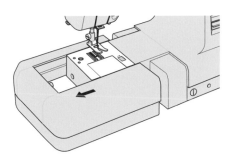

Auto thread

A semi auto-thread function that threads the needle for you will save time if you are new to sewing or if your eyesight is not perfect. A small hook located behind the needle pulls the thread through the eye as the hook is withdrawn (see Using an Auto Threader, page 39, for more details). The auto threader works best on threads of average thickness – very thick or specialist threads will almost certainly need threading by hand.

The spool pin for the thread is either right on top of the machine at the right-hand end, or set on a shelf just behind the body. On some models, the spool pins can be retracted when not in use.

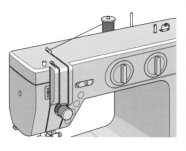

On some machines the spool pin may be set horizontally, and may be concealed inside a hinged section of the body.

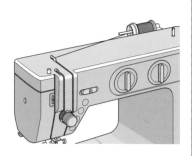

THE BOBBIN THREAD

The bobbin holds the lower thread and sits under the needle plate. Bobbins can be top-loading or side/front-loading. A top-loading bobbin is dropped into the machine through a sliding or lifting panel in the needle plate (see page 35). A side/front-loading bobbin is placed into a bobbin case, which is then inserted into the machine through a door in the front or the side of the flat bed (see page 35).

Lockstitch

Most modern domestic sewing machines perform lockstitch, in which one thread comes down through the needle and a second thread comes up from the bobbin. The needle (or top) thread and bobbin thread each stay on their own side of the fabric, but if the tension is correct, they interlock in the middle of the layers of fabric, creating a secure stitch that looks the same on both sides (for more on thread tension, see page 40).

FABRIC FEED

The fabric is normally fed through the sewing machine by the drop feed mechanism. When the needle moves upwards and withdraws from the fabric, the feed dog comes up through slots in the needle plate and the serrated top surface grips the material, which is held firmly against it by the presser foot. The feed dog moves horizontally backwards, so the fabric is dragged backwards into position for the next stitch. The feed dog is then lowered again and returns to its original position while the needle makes its next pass through the fabric. While the needle is in the fabric, there is no feed action.

Lowering or covering the feed dog

When doing some kinds of stitching it is better to be able to move the fabric around freely under the needle, instead of allowing the feed dog to move it automatically as you stitch. If you are planning to use your sewing machine for free-motion quilting, machine

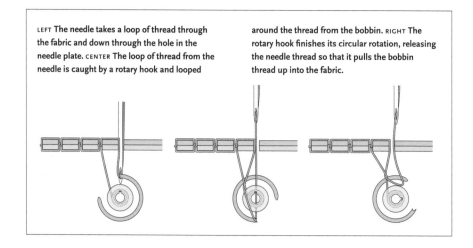

LEFT The needle takes a loop of thread through the fabric and down through the hole in the needle plate. CENTER The loop of thread from the needle is caught by a rotary hook and looped around the thread from the bobbin. RIGHT The rotary hook finishes its circular rotation, releasing the needle thread so that it pulls the bobbin thread up into the fabric.

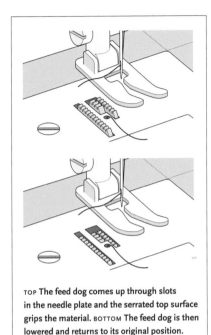

TOP The feed dog comes up through slots in the needle plate and the serrated top surface grips the material. BOTTOM The feed dog is then lowered and returns to its original position.

embroidery or darning, you will need to be able to put the feed dog out of action by dropping or covering it (see page 31).

Dual feed

As you sew, the feed dog pulls the fabric through the machine. When sewing together two layers of fabric, the fabric layer next to the feed dog will tend to move at a slightly faster rate than the upper layer. When stitching most fabrics this speed difference is usually unnoticeable, but if you are stitching multiple layers or very slippery fabrics, or if you require very precise pattern matching – on plaids, for instance – the discrepancy may become an issue.

A dual feed system is designed to move the top and bottom fabric layers at the same rate, so eliminating slippage. Dual feed may be built in,

usually as a second foot that can be lowered behind the presser foot to pull the top fabric layer along in tandem with the feed dog pulling the lower fabric layer. When not in use, the dual feed can be pushed up behind the machine out of the way. If there is no built-in dual feed system, you may be able to buy a special presser foot – called a dual feed foot, even-feed foot, or walking foot – with its own feed dog that has a similar function.

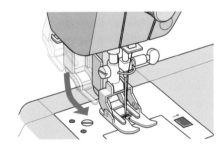

Some machines – particularly models aimed at quiltmakers – have a built-in dual feed system.

PRESSER FEET

The presser foot is a shaped piece of metal or plastic with a hole through which the needle stitches. It sits below the needle and holds the fabric securely against the feed dog as the machine stitches. It can be raised when you want to slide the fabric under the needle, then lowered again to hold the fabric against the needle plate (see Presser Feet Techniques, page 30).

The presser foot can be removed completely quite easily if you want to change to a different type for a special task (see Types of Presser Foot, page 28).

Knee lifter

A knee lifter is a long bar with a bend that slots into the front of a machine and extends down next to the knee. It allows you to lift and lower the presser foot with your knee, so leaving both hands free to manipulate the fabric.

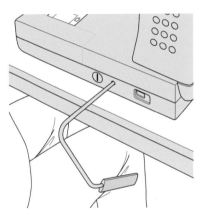

The knee lifter allows you to lift and lower the presser foot with your knee. However, on some machines a similar bar is an alternative to the foot pedal and controls the speed of stitching instead.

Automatic and adjustable foot pressure

If a machine has automatic foot pressure it will automatically adjust to the thickness of the item being sewn. This may work well across mid-range thicknesses, but it may not handle very bulky or very thin fabrics successfully. A machine with adjustable foot pressure will allow you to reduce the pressure when sewing very thin fabrics or to increase it when stitching through many layers – such as when quiltmaking or making home décor projects – which will give better results.

STITCH SELECTOR

Most modern machines come with a range of basic stitches, including straight stitches, several different types of zigzag stitch, a buttonhole function, one or more stretch stitches for stretchy fabrics, and maybe even a couple of decorative stitches. On some inexpensive machines the length and width are preset for each stitch pattern and cannot be varied. In other cases, only the length can be varied. The ability to select the stitch type, length and width separately is a better option for anyone who wants to sew more than a straight stitch and will allow you to adjust each stitch to suit the type of fabric being sewn. If you plan to do a lot of dressmaking, a wider selection of different types of buttonhole will be useful, and for even the simplest decorative stitching you will need a good range of embroidery stitches.

Three basic types

Different manufacturers handle the exact details of stitch selection in a slightly different way, but there are three basic types of stitch selector.
Pattern discs: some older models of electric sewing machine have pattern discs that are slotted into the machine, with one disc for each pattern.
Number or letter dial: most electric machines have a numbered or lettered dial, with each setting corresponding to a different stitch pattern. The dial can show only a limited number of patterns, but sometimes it can also be used in conjunction with a special setting on the stitch width or length dial, which allows twice the number of patterns to be offered.

LCD display screen: even the most basic computerized machine has too many patterns for a simple dial. Each pattern is illustrated with its own reference number and a stitch is selected by keying in the number, which appears on the LCD screen. Machines that have hundreds of patterns usually have them arranged in groups, so you begin by selecting the group, and then key in the specific pattern number.

The buttonhole function

There are two types of automatic buttonhole function: the four-step and the one-step. On the four-step, two stitch patterns make up the buttonhole, one close zigzag to stitch the sides and one long zigzag to make a bar tack at each end. It is called a four-step because you change between these two patterns to stitch the two sides and the two ends. With the one-step buttonhole, a button is placed in a holder on the special presser foot to set the size of the buttonhole, which is then stitched automatically from start to finish (see page 99).

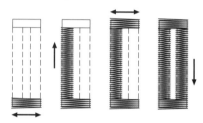

The four-step buttonhole.

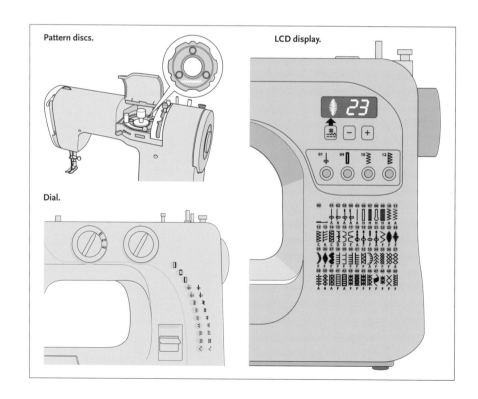

Pattern discs.

LCD display.

Dial.

THE RIGHT MACHINE

Before you look for a machine, decide what sort of tasks you want to do and set a rough budget based on the amount of sewing you will undertake. If the machine will be used only occasionally, do not spend extra money for lots of fancy stitches and accessories that you will never need.

BEGINNER, INTERMEDIATE OR EXPERT?

If you are learning to sew, or only want to stitch the occasional seam, you just need an inexpensive machine with a range of basic stitches, such as straight stitch, a few different zigzags and a buttonhole function. However, if you plan to develop your skills, you will soon need a bigger range of stitches, functions and accessories, and you will benefit from a machine that makes repetitive tasks, such as stitching a buttonhole and finishing off seam allowances, as simple as possible. Extra stitches and functions cannot be added later to the more basic machines, so think ahead. An already experienced sewer will probably require many more features to begin with and maybe some special functions, such as dual feed, adjustable bobbin tension or the ability to compose and store embroidery patterns, so a computerized model may be worth the extra investment. Take a look at the flow chart below to determine what type of machine matches your sewing skill.

Be realistic in your needs and look for a good basic machine with the minimum functions you require for your skill level. Consider also what kind of tasks you will be using your machine for. For general home sewing, repairs and alterations a standard machine will be quite adequate, but if there is a particular area of sewing you are interested in there may be special features you should look for (see pages 20–21).

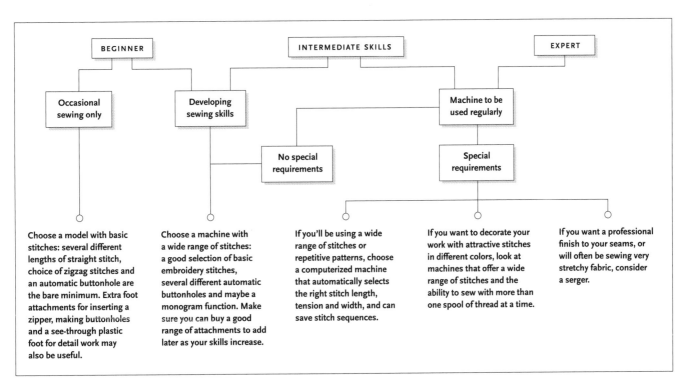

BEGINNER

INTERMEDIATE SKILLS

EXPERT

Occasional sewing only

Developing sewing skills

Machine to be used regularly

No special requirements

Special requirements

Choose a model with basic stitches: several different lengths of straight stitch, choice of zigzag stitches and an automatic buttonhole are the bare minimum. Extra foot attachments for inserting a zipper, making buttonholes and a see-through plastic foot for detail work may also be useful.

Choose a machine with a wide range of stitches: a good selection of basic embroidery stitches, several different automatic buttonholes and maybe a monogram function. Make sure you can buy a good range of attachments to add later as your skills increase.

If you'll be using a wide range of stitches or repetitive patterns, choose a computerized machine that automatically selects the right stitch length, tension and width, and can save stitch sequences.

If you want to decorate your work with attractive stitches in different colors, look at machines that offer a wide range of stitches and the ability to sew with more than one spool of thread at a time.

If you want a professional finish to your seams, or will often be sewing very stretchy fabric, consider a serger.

THE DRESSMAKER

The more complex the garments you want to make, the more likely it is you will need a machine with a wide range of features. Look for the following:

Free arm: for easier sewing of sleeves and pant legs. Some flat bed machines can be converted to free arm when required by removing a section of the bed.

Serger stitch: used to neaten seams and hems for a professional look, but if this stitch takes the machine out of your budget range, you can use a close-set zigzag stitch instead (see page 53).

Automatic buttonholes: choose a machine with a one-step buttonhole function (see page 99); the ability to stitch more than one design of buttonhole will be useful.

Presser feet: a zigzag foot, blind hem foot, concealed zipper foot and rolled hem foot should come as standard or be available as extras.

Adjustable foot pressure: this allows you to reduce the pressure of the foot against the feed dog when sewing delicate or stretchy fabrics.

▼ The free arm makes stitching narrow cylindrical items easier, and the removable section of the flat bed often doubles up as a storage box.

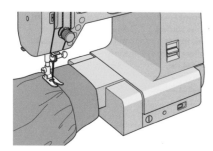

THE QUILTMAKER

The larger the backward C-shaped opening between the needle and the control side of the machine, the easier it will be to machine-quilt large quilts. Many machines have a range of special attachments to make patchwork and quilting easier. Look for the following:

Drop feed dog: if you plan to free-motion machine quilt, you will need a machine in which the feed dog can be dropped out of the way or covered (see page 31).

Adjustable bobbin case: for good results when free-motion quilting you may need to adjust the tension on the bobbin thread. On some machines this will invalidate the warranty, so make sure you can buy a special bobbin case for free-motion work or a spare bobbin case that you can adjust as necessary

▶ It is important to support large pieces of work as much as possible while you stitch, partly because it makes it much easier to sew but also because the weight of fabric pulling to one side could pull the stitching off line or bend the needle. So, if you are intending to make quilts or drapes with your machine, an extension table is essential.

(see page 41), leaving the original at its factory settings. If you buy a spare bobbin case for tension adjustments, make sure you mark it so you can tell it apart from the original.

Extension table: to attach to the needle side of the machine when working on large quilts.

Presser feet: a walking foot, ditch quilting foot, appliqué foot, open-toe free-motion quilting foot, quarter-inch quilting/patchwork foot may all prove useful.

Adjustable foot pressure: for working with delicate fabrics or for doing appliqué work.

Electronic speed limiter: this allows you to set the maximum speed that the machine will stitch with the foot control fully depressed. It gives you better control when quilting or sewing around curves and corners.

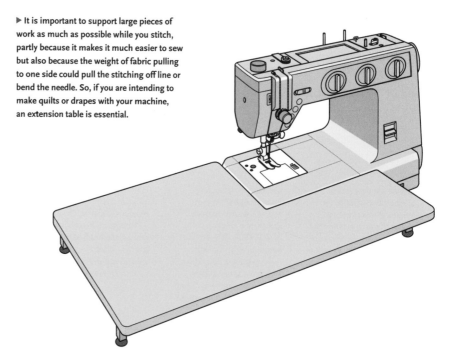

THE HOME DÉCOR MAKER

For home decorating projects you will probably be using heavier fabrics, so you will need a sturdy machine that can cope with such heavy-duty work easily. Look for the following:

Presser feet: a blind hem foot and a concealed zipper foot will be useful, and you should consider buying a piping foot, gathering foot and ruffle foot if you are going to carry out these tasks regularly.

Adjustable stitch length: most modern machines offer some kind of facility to adjust the stitch, but make sure that there is a separate width and length control and that the stitch length offered covers a good range. Heavyweight upholstery fabrics need a much longer stitch length as standard than lightweight dressmaking fabrics.

Adjustable foot pressure: for working with bulky fabrics.

Extension table: to support drapes, bedspreads, or other large projects properly as you sew.

THE EMBELLISHING MACHINE

✂ The embellishing machine uses the needle-punch felting technique to produce decorative motifs on fabrics.

✂ It has several barbed needles set in a circle that move as one unit, catching fibers to mesh them together.

✂ Scraps of fabric, yarn or threads are laid on top of a base fabric and beneath the needles. Depressing the foot pedal activates the needles.

✂ It is ideal for decoration and for making 3D embellishments, but it will not sew a conventional seam.

THE EMBROIDERER

If you plan to do a lot of machine embroidery, consider a computerized machine or a specialist embroidery machine, both of which will have a wide range of pre-programed patterns. Look for the following:

Multi-spool ability: to deal with several colors of thread simultaneously.

CD or card slot, or USB port: to enable you to purchase and add extra stitches and patterns at a later date.

Computer compatibility: to allow you to connect to the Internet via computer to download further stitch programs and to use design software.

Memory function: so you can store frequently used sequences of stitches. Check how many sequences the machine will allow you to store.

Adjustable foot pressure: for working with delicate fabrics.

Drop feed dog function: for free-motion embroidery the feed dog must be able to be dropped out of the way or covered (see page 31).

The embellisher is great for making trims and adding decorative touches, but it cannot be used for general sewing.

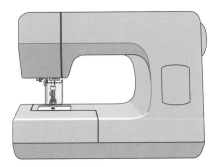

OTHER FACTORS TO CONSIDER

As well as your budget, your skill level, and the sewing tasks you are likely to perform on your machine, there are a few other considerations for choosing the right machine for you.

Transportability

If you want to take your machine around with you to classes or to sewing bees, or if you need to pack it up and put it away after each use, check how much it weighs. Lifting or carrying a very heavy machine will quickly become a chore.

Storage

It is important to keep your machine free of dust when it is not being used and many machines come with a dust protector of some sort. A soft cover is the cheapest option; it is perfectly adequate for covering machines that will be left in position when not in use. A hard cover is more expensive but is a better choice for machines that have to be stored away or moved around between sewing sessions. On some machines the hard cover is designed to fold down from the sides to form a useful extension to the sewing area.

Aftercare

If you buy your machine from a large department store or independent retailer, ask if they offer free sewing lessons as part of the deal. Also make sure you get a good warranty with a new machine. Check the arrangements for servicing and repair, how long the normal turnaround is, and if it is possible to borrow a machine while yours is out of action.

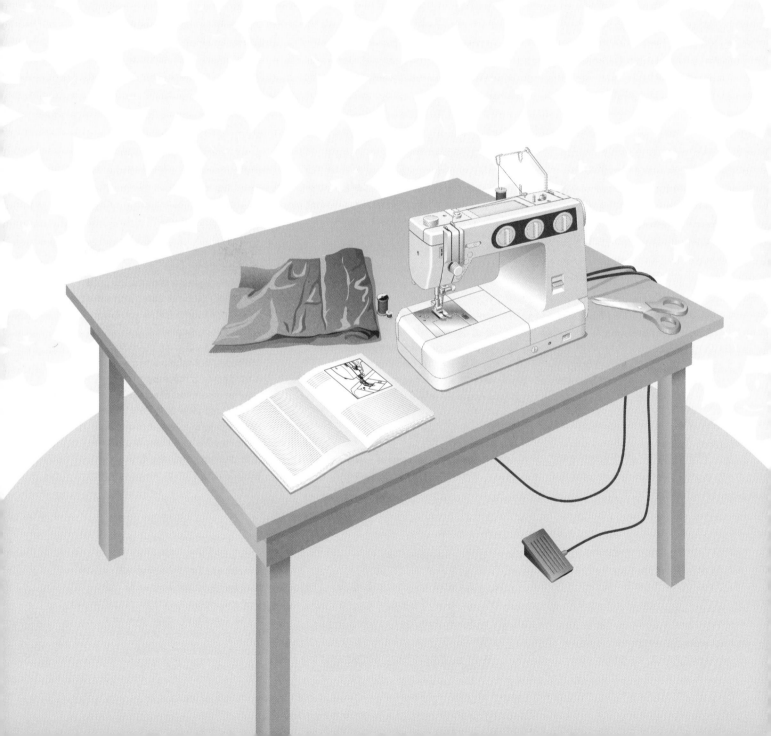

KNOWING YOUR MACHINE

Now that you have chosen your sewing machine, you will be eager to get it home and begin work on your first project straightaway. But take some time to set up a dedicated place to sew and get to know how your particular sewing machine works, trying out the different settings, speeds and attachments. This chapter has instructions and diagrams for all the basic functions that are common to most machines, but it's always worth checking your machine's manual too as some options will vary across different makes and models.

A PLACE TO SEW

Some sewing projects may take a while to complete, and in an ideal world you would have a space where you could leave everything spread out so you could pick up where you left off each time. If this is not possible, find a place to set up your machine so that you will be comfortable while working.

GOOD POSTURE

When working at the sewing machine for long periods, your forearms should be at a 90-degree angle to your body and the sewing bed should be at the same level as the bottom of your elbows. To achieve this you might need a higher chair or a lower table than normal. Your wrists should be resting approximately midway between your waist and chest. To avoid neck or back strain and to allow ease of movement, a chair with a straight back and no arms is best. Plug in the foot control and position it near your right foot. If your machine is operated by a knee bar rather than a foot control, position this so it comes down next to your right knee.

Take some time to be sure you are comfortable because working in an awkward position for long periods will soon lead to backache.

GOOD LIGHTING

Do not underestimate the importance of good lighting. Most sewing machines have a built-in light that comes on as soon as the machine is switched on, shining on the needle plate. However, you will also need an additional light source to illuminate the surrounding area. A flexible table lamp that can be positioned as required is the best option. A daylight lamp is very useful if color-matching fabrics is particularly important to your project, or for embroidery and other colored hand-stitching work.

TIP When replacing built-in light bulbs, make sure the replacement bulb is the same type, voltage and wattage as the old one.

STORING YOUR MACHINE

Always cover your machine with its soft cover or hard case when it is not in use, to keep it clean and dust-free. You can then store it in any convenient dry place, such as under a table or in the back of a wardrobe.

CARE AND MAINTENANCE

Most modern machines are designed to be as maintenance-free as possible, but they should be cleaned regularly to prevent dust and residue produced by fabric and thread from building up, as this will lead to excess wear and tear. Get in the habit of cleaning all the lint out of your machine every time you finish a project, paying particular attention to the area under the needle plate around the feed dog and bobbin mechanism. Remove the needle plate or open the access panel; take out the bobbin and then the bobbin holder;

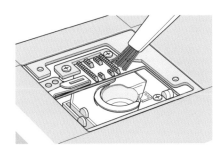

Cleaning the lint on a top-loading bobbin case. Use the small, stiff lint brush that came with your machine and pay particular attention to the feed dog (shown) and the hook race in front.

use the small, stiff lint brush that came with your machine to clean the lint and fluff from the bobbin holder, and from between the feed dog and hook race.

Many modern machines do not need oiling, so check the manual first. If oil is required, the manual will show exactly where to put it and on some older machines the lubrication points may even be marked in the machine itself. Always make sure you use an oil specifically designed for sewing machines. Oiling the machine not only lubricates moving parts to prevent wear, but also reduces the risk of rust. Rust can form rapidly, even just from humidity in the air, and creates a grainy surface that will lead to excess wear. After oiling, make a few lines of stitching on some scrap fabric before working on a project to allow any excess oil to escape.

Servicing

If the machine is still within its guarantee period, servicing should be carried out by an approved technician in accordance with the manufacturer's warranty terms. After the guarantee has lapsed, the choice of service engineer is more flexible, but it is important to make sure that whoever you choose is a qualified technician, especially in the case of computerized machines. If you use your machine very heavily – at least five times a week – then it should be serviced once a year. For moderate to light usage – on average less than once a week – service your machine every two years. Even if you don't use your machine very often, it should be serviced occasionally. Always send the machine for a service if it has been dropped or damaged, has become wet, or has jammed up completely.

STORAGE SOLUTIONS

✂ Store small pieces of fabric in lidded plastic see-through crates. These can be stacked to take up less room, and you will be able to see the contents without unpacking.

✂ Store large lengths of fabric on cardboard rolls in a cupboard: avoid folding as the weight of the layers will produce creases over time that can be hard to remove.

✂ Hang up garments and drapes under construction between work sessions so that they do not crease. To prevent marking the fabric, pad the crossbar of a hanger before draping fabric over it.

✂ Keep quilt blocks flat until you are ready to join them up into a quilt top by stacking them on a shelf or in a box.

✂ Keep small pieces of miscellaneous sewing equipment in transparent storage containers so you can see what you have at a glance. Choose a type with separate compartments or drawers so that the different items can be kept apart and found easily.

✂ Store spools of thread in a storage box to keep them clean and to prevent the ends from tangling together. Larger cones of thread can be stored on racks specially made for that purpose.

✂ Keep a wound bobbin and matching spool of thread together by threading a length of string through the central hole of both and knotting the ends together.

✂ Keep storage crates and boxes, and the sewing machine, together in a dedicated cupboard.

SEWING MACHINE ANATOMY

When you first get your sewing machine, take some time to study the manual to check where all the parts are and what the various buttons and levers do. The illustrations on the following pages will help you to find your way around your machine, although the actual location and configuration of some of these features may vary, depending on the make and model of your machine.

FRONT

1 **Foot pressure dial:** to adjust foot pressure when sewing lightweight or heavyweight fabrics or bulky layers; however, a machine with automatic foot pressure will be adequate for the average sewing project.

2 **Thread take-up lever:** moves up and down with the needle and controls the amount of thread needed for stitching.

3 **Bobbin thread guide with tension disc:** to take the thread from the spool to the bobbin winding spindle. This guide has a tension disc so the bobbin thread is wound tightly.

4 **Speed control:** this enables you to limit the maximum stitching speed for more even stitching.

5 **Thread guides:** there are several of these along the threading run to take the thread in the right direction.

6 **Bobbin winder spindle:** used when filling up the bobbin with thread.

7 **Stitch width dial:** controls the distance the needle moves from side to side when sewing zigzag or other decorative stitches.

8 **Stitch length dial:** for adjusting the length of your stitches – a machine that

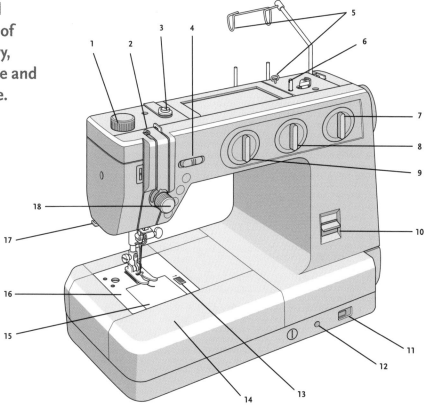

allows a good range of stitch lengths will be more versatile in the long run.

9 Stitch selector dial: used to select the machine's built-in stitches.

10 Reverse stitch lever: allows you to sew in reverse. On some models reverse stitch is selected by turning the stitch length dial (8) to a minus number.

11 Drop feed lever: lowers the feed dog below the needle plate to put it out of action when free-motion sewing. Alternatively, it may be possible to temporarily fix a plate over the feed dog.

12 Knee lifter socket: where the knee lifter (if one is provided) plugs in.

13 Hook cover release button: releases the hook cover plate to access the bobbin (top-loading machines only).

14 Flat bed: a large flat sewing area. On some machines part of this may detach to reveal the free arm.

15 Hook cover plate: covers the bobbin in its casing (only found on a top-loading bobbin machine).

16 Needle plate: marked with common seam allowances as a guide to accurate sewing. It can be removed by unfastening tiny screws to clean the bobbin casing, feed dog and hook race.

17 Thread cutter: for cutting the needle thread.

18 Tension dial: used to adjust the tension of the needle thread for a perfectly balanced stitch.

BACK

19 Foot control socket: connect the plug here for the foot pedal that controls the stitching speed.

20 Power switch: turns the power and the machine's built-in sewing light on or off.

21 Hand wheel: turning the hand wheel raises and lowers the needle. Always turn the hand wheel counter-clockwise.

22 Thread cutter: used to cut the bobbin thread when the bobbin is fully wound.

23 Bobbin winder stopper: this is pushed against the bobbin when winding begins. When the bobbin is full it pops back and stops the bobbin winding mechanism.

24 Carrying handle: always carry the machine by its handle.

25 Thread spool pins: these hold the thread for the needle and can be set vertically or horizontally.

26 Presser foot lifting lever: lift to slide the fabric beneath, or when changing the presser foot. For more detail, see page 28.

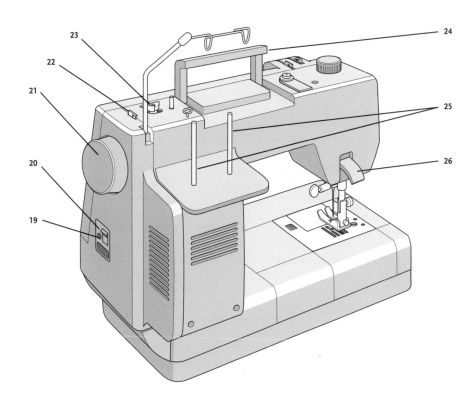

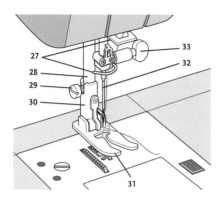

PRESSER FOOT DETAIL

27 Thread guides: take the needle thread towards the eye of the needle.

28 Presser bar: the foot holder clips around this, held in place by the thumbscrew.

29 Presser foot thumbscrew: releases the entire presser foot holder.

30 Presser foot holder: clips onto the presser bar – on some machines the foot and the foot holder are all one piece.

31 Presser foot: holds the fabric firmly against the needle plate and feed dog so that the stitches form properly.

32 Needle: the needle takes the upper thread through the fabric and down through the needle plate. For details of needle types, see page 34.

33 Needle clamp screw: loosen to remove a needle; tighten to secure a needle in position.

PRESSER FEET

The presser foot on a sewing machine holds the fabric firmly against the needle plate while the stitch is formed. It can easily be changed and there are many different types of foot available for different tasks.

TYPES OF PRESSER FOOT

Your sewing machine will almost certainly come with a few basic presser feet – usually a standard or zigzag foot, a zipper foot and maybe a buttonhole foot – and these will be all that you need to begin with, but as your skills develop

you might want to invest in some special feet. The names given here may vary slightly depending on the manufacturer, and not all of them will be available on every make or model.

Appliqué or satin stitch foot: this clear plastic foot is perfect to see through when embroidering or for easy maneuvering when sewing appliqué pieces. It may be hinged for extra maneuverability.

Bias binder foot: this foot will fold under the edges of flat bias tape for quick and easy binding of raw edges.

Blind hem foot: the guide on this foot helps to feed the fabric and create a straight and nearly invisible blind hem.

Buttonhole foot: this is useful for machine-stitched buttonholes, although many modern machines have an automatic program enabling you to stitch buttonholes using the general presser foot. An **automatic buttonhole foot** has a special attachment that holds the button and sizes the buttonhole automatically to fit (see page 99).

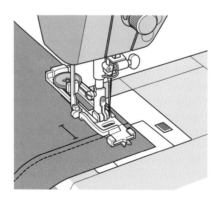

Automatic buttonhole foot.

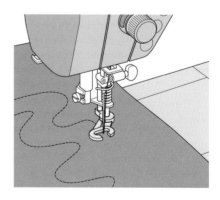

Darning foot.

Cording foot: designed to hold one or more strands of cording as you stitch.

Craft foot: a clear plastic foot with an open toe for patchwork and appliqué.

Darning foot: also known as the quilting, embroidery or appliqué foot, this has a small round or C-shaped end so very little of the stitching area is obscured. It is often used with the feed dog down for greater control of stitching direction.

Ditch quilting foot: a foot with an extended guide at the front to help you to stay on the line of the seam as the machine stitches.

Dual feed foot: this foot is used when stitching hard-to-feed fabrics, and prevents them from shifting and puckering. It is ideal when you need to match patterns across a seam perfectly. Some machines have a dual feed foot built in as standard. See also Walking or even-feed foot.

Gathering foot: this gathers lightweight and medium fabrics as you stitch. See also Ruffle or pleater foot.

Open-toe free-motion quilting foot: a foot with the front removed for clearer visibility when sewing free-motion.

Overcasting foot: a specially designed foot which simulates the look of a professional overlock seam; it has wires to prevent the fabric edge from puckering or rolling.

Pin tuck foot: the ridges on the underside of this foot pull the fabric into a series of small tucks, which can then be stitched in neat and even lines. It is always used with a twin needle (see page 53).

Piping foot: this foot is ideal for making and applying corded piping.

Quarter-inch seam foot: allows you to sew a ¼in (6mm) seam allowance quickly and accurately. It may have a guide on it to prevent the fabric from going past the edge and is sometimes known as a 'little foot'.

Rolled or narrow hem foot: this has a special curled piece of metal at the front, which turns the edge of light and medium-weight fabrics under to create a double folded hem as you stitch.

Ruffle or pleater foot: this is used to create perfectly even ruffles or pleats in lightweight fabrics. See also Gathering foot.

Teflon foot: a nonstick foot which glides over difficult fabric surfaces, improving the stitch quality in many problem fabrics, such as hook-and-loop tapes, leather and vinyl.

Walking or even-feed foot: this foot draws the top and bottom layers of fabric along at the same speed, preventing multiple layers or very slippery fabrics from being pushed out of alignment by the action of the feed dog. See also Dual feed foot and the section on Dual feed on page 17.

Zigzag foot: an all-purpose foot that can be used for zigzag or straight stitch.

Zipper foot: this narrow foot slides down the side of the zipper teeth instead of straddling them. It is also useful for inserting piping into a seam. A **concealed** or **invisible zipper foot** is a special type of zipper foot used to insert concealed zippers.

Gathering foot.

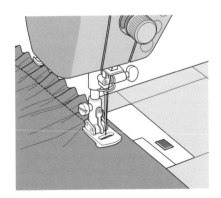

Rolled hem foot.

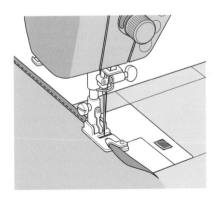

Walking foot.

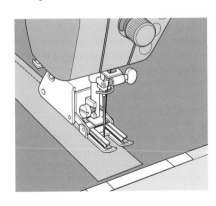

PRESSER FEET TECHNIQUES

Spend a little time getting to know how the presser foot attachments work on the sewing machine model you have. Become familiar with what each foot can do by practicing on scraps of fabric.

Raising and lowering

You raise and lower the presser foot by pushing up or down on the presser foot-lifting lever. This can be found near the needle, usually either at the back or the side of the machine.

Removing and replacing a clip-on fitting

On some machines the presser foot is a clip-on fitting: the foot is a separate part with a bar at the top that clips onto the bottom of the foot holder. These instructions are for removing the foot section only. For some replacement feet it may be necessary to remove both the foot and the foot holder. To do so, follow the instructions for removing and replacing a screw-on fitting, right.

A1 To remove the foot section only, raise the presser foot lifter and press the button on the rear of the foot holder; the foot will drop off.

A2 Place the replacement foot on the needle plate, lining it up so the bar is under the clip on the foot holder. Lower the presser foot lifter until the foot holder clips onto the foot.

PRESSER FEET

✄ While some presser feet can be used for a variety of tasks, some have a very specific function. Investing in a good range of presser feet will allow you to get the most from your sewing machine.

✄ Presser feet are either a clip-on or screw-on fitting and both are easy to replace.

✄ If the presser foot is a screw-on type, it may have a long holder or a short one (also known as a long or short shaft). You need to be aware what type fits your machine when buying additional feet.

✄ Generic non-branded feet may fit your machine as well as those made specifically for it.

✄ Presser feet designed for free-motion work are often spring loaded so they go up and down with the needle.

✄ When fitting a spring-loaded foot with an arm at the top, the arm needs to sit above the needle clamp screw. Try squeezing the foot to compress the spring a little as you fit it to the presser foot bar, sliding the spring-loaded arm over the needle clamp screw.

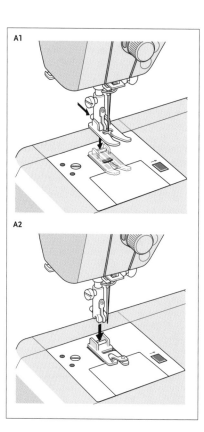

A1

A2

Removing and replacing a screw-on fitting

If the presser foot is a screw-on fitting, the foot and the foot holder are one piece and the top of the foot holder fits around one side of the presser bar, held in place with a thumbscrew. To release the foot holder and presser foot together, loosen the thumbscrew, with a screwdriver if necessary, until you can slide the whole presser foot out. It is not usually necessary to take the thumbscrew right out to do this. Note, the machine's foot holder may look different than the one illustrated, but the basic principle should be the same.

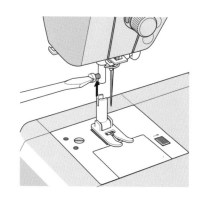

Altering the presser foot pressure

On some machines it is possible to change the pressure exerted by the presser foot, by turning a dial that is usually situated on top or on the side of the machine at the needle end. For most sewing the pressure should be set at the normal setting – on some machines this is indicated by an N, on others it is 0 or 3, so check the machine manual before making changes.

Reduce the pressure slightly for appliqué, embroidery and darning. For fine fabrics, such as chiffon and lace, reduce the pressure further to its lowest point. For bulky fabric or thick layers, increase the foot pressure.

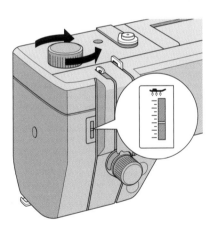

TIP Incorrect presser foot pressure can cause the layers of the fabric to slip out of alignment as you sew. If this is happening, check you haven't adjusted the pressure for a previous project and forgotten to turn it back to normal afterwards.

THE FEED DOG

The feed dog automatically feeds the fabric under the presser foot as you stitch. For free-motion work you need to be able to move the fabric around under the needle at will, and this is achieved by putting the feed dog out of action, either by dropping it or by covering it with a plate. The feed dog also needs to be out of action for some other functions, such as sewing on buttons.

Dropping the feed dog

When the feed dog is dropped it still operates, but below the level of the needle plate so it is not able to move the fabric. If the machine has the facility to drop the feed dog, this is done by moving a slider, pulling down on a lever or turning a knob on the base of the machine; the exact position of the control varies from model to model. It may be marked with a double or triple triangle symbol with a horizontal line – the version with the top points of the triangle below the line indicates the feed dog dropped position, the version with the line running through the centre of the triangles indicates the feed dog raised position.

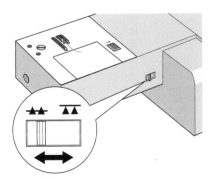

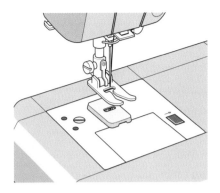

Covering the feed dog

On some machines it is not possible to lower the feed dog, but it may be covered with a metal or plastic plate. This clips into place on the needle plate over the feed dog slots; the feed dog still operates underneath but cannot grip the fabric. The cover plate has a central slot for the needle to go through as normal.

Raising the feed dog

If you have dropped the feed dog and want to raise it again, just moving the slider or lever back is often not enough to bring it back into action instantly. You may also need to turn the hand wheel completely round once, or press the up/down needle button, before the feed dog will engage properly. When you can see the feed dog coming up through the needle plate, it is safe to resume normal stitching again.

NEEDLES

The needle carries the upper thread down to meet the lower thread, so it needs to be heavy enough to pierce the fabric but not so big that it leaves an unsightly hole. A worn, dull or damaged needle can cause stitch problems, such as skipped stitches or puckering seams (see Troubleshooting, page 56).

NEEDLES

✂ As a guide, you should put a fresh needle into the machine at the beginning of each major project or after six to eight hours of sewing.

✂ Change the sewing machine needle regularly and always use good-quality needles.

✂ If the needle has a flat side on the shank, make sure it is inserted into the clamp the right way round.

✂ Most modern machines have the flat side to the rear, but for older machines, check the manual.

✂ Alternatively, slide a small hand mirror under the bottom of the clamp to check if one side of the hole is flat.

✂ A few machines use fully round needles instead of the flat-sided type. The two types are not interchangeable, so make sure you replace the needle with the correct type for your machine.

NEEDLE ANATOMY

The fatter top of the needle that fits into the needle clamp is called the shank. The shank of most modern needles has a round front and flat back to ensure that the needle is fitted the correct way round. The shaft is below the shank – the size of the needle is determined by the shaft's thickness. The point is the tip of the needle that pierces the fabric and the eye is the hole through which the thread is passed. As the point of the needle makes a hole through the fabric the thread slides into a long groove that runs up one side of the shaft from the eye, so the hole made is only the same diameter as the needle. On the back of the needle there is a short groove – the scarf – just above the eye, which allows the shuttle or hook to pick up the needle thread to form the stitch.

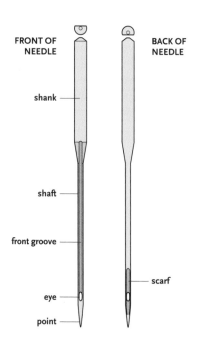

FRONT OF NEEDLE — BACK OF NEEDLE

shank
shaft
front groove
scarf
eye
point

Removing and replacing the needle

The needle is held in place by a screw clamp, so it is very easy to remove without any special tools.

A1 Raise the presser foot and take hold of the needle between finger and thumb. Loosen the needle by turning the screw clamp – usually counterclockwise – then slide the needle down and out at an angle. As you do so, note if the needle

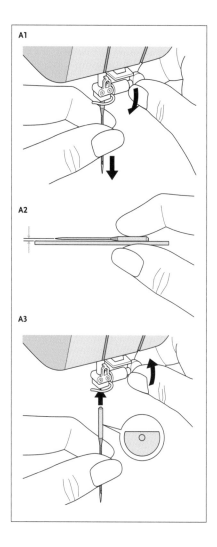

A1

A2

A3

has a flat side on its shank and if so whether this was facing to the rear or to the front.

A2 To check that the replacement needle is straight before fitting, put it on a perfectly flat and smooth surface and hold it in place at the shank. The gap between the needle and the surface should be consistent, from the point, along the shaft to the shank.

A3 To replace the needle, with the presser foot still up, slide the end of the needle into the clamp. If the needle has a flat side, make sure that this is facing in the same direction as the old needle. Tighten the screw clamp firmly so the needle stays in place.

Needle position

When stitching straight stitches the needle normally drops down through the center of the presser foot slot, but on many machines the needle drop position can be changed so it stitches to the left or the right of center. This means you can position the line of stitching exactly without taking the fabric out from under the presser foot, which is very useful when doing some types of sewing, such as topstitching and inserting zippers. To change the needle drop position, select a straight stitch style and adjust the stitch width until the needle drops where you want it.

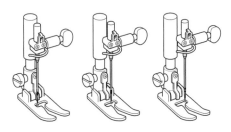

TYPES OF NEEDLE

There was only one type of needle available for early sewing machines and the only choice was in size. Nowadays, however, there is such a wide variety of needle types available that it can be hard to determine which one to use. Factors affecting the choice of needle are the fabric being sewn, the thread being used, and the type of stitch being worked. For general sewing, the fabric type determines the shape of the needle point and the fabric weight determines the needle size. Learn more about the different needle choices available to you below; then use the handy fabric/needle chart on page 34 to help you to select the right needle for the project in hand.

Ballpoint and stretch needles: the ballpoint needle is used for heavy, loose knits, and the stretch needle for elastic fabrics, such as Lycra. Both types have rounded points that will slide between the fabric threads rather than piercing them, but the tip of the ballpoint is slightly more rounded than that of the stretch needle. When working on a knit fabric, if the ballpoint needle results in skipped stitches, try the stretch needle.

Denim (jeans) needle: suitable for working on heavyweight denim, this needle is also great for duck, canvas, upholstery fabrics, artificial leather, and vinyl. It has a deeper scarf, a long, sharp point, and modified shaft so it doesn't push the fabric down into the needle-plate hole. It works best on densely woven fabrics, but if stitches are skipped when sewing very heavy fabrics, try a larger needle and sew more slowly or walk the needle through the fabric by turning the hand wheel.

Embroidery needle: used for machine embroidery or embellishing with decorative thread, this needle has a medium-sharp point – between a sharp and a ballpoint – and an enlarged eye to keep decorative threads from shredding or breaking and to prevent skipped stitches. If the thread shreds on dense or heavily stitched designs, use a larger size needle or a Metallica needle.

Hemstitch or wing needle: specifically for hemstitching or heirloom embroidery on linen and batiste, this needle has fins on the sides of the shank to create holes as you sew. The stitch is more effective when the needle returns to the same needle hole more than once. If the needle pushes the fabric into the needle hole, place stabilizer under the fabric.

Leather needle: the sewing point of this needle is shaped a little like an arrowhead, so it is perfect for cutting through natural leather.

Metallic, Metafil and Metallica needles: these needles are designed for sewing with decorative metallic threads. They have a universal or standard point, an elongated eye and a large groove to allow fragile metallic and synthetic filament threads to flow smoothly.

Microtex and sharp needles: these have a very sharp point and are used on microfiber, silk and synthetic leather, but they are also perfect for stitching precise edges and heirloom sewing. It may help to use a rolled, even- or dual feed presser foot.

Quilting or stippling needle: used for piecing, quilting, and stippling, it has a tapered shaft to avoid fabric damage when stitching multiple layers. Move the fabric smoothly – without pulling on the needle – when free-motion stitching to avoid breaking the needle.

FABRIC TYPE	THREAD	NEEDLE TYPE	NEEDLE SIZE US/UK
Delicate: tulle, chiffon, fine lace, organza	Fine mercerized cotton, fine synthetic thread, silk	Universal, Microtex or sharp	9/65
Lightweight: batiste, organdie, jersey, voile, taffeta, crêpe, chiffon, velvet, plastic film, silk	Medium mercerized cotton, synthetic thread, silk	Universal, Microtex or sharp	11/75
Medium-weight: gingham, percale, piqué, linen, chintz, faille, satin, fine corduroy, velvet, suiting, knits, deep-pile fabrics, vinyl	Medium mercerized cotton, cotton, synthetic thread, silk	Universal	14/90
Medium-heavy: gaberdine, tweed, sailcloth, denim, furnishing fabrics, synthetic leather	Heavy-duty mercerized cotton, cotton, synthetic thread	Universal, denim, Microtex or sharp	16/100
Heavy: overcoatings, canvas, heavy upholstery fabrics	Heavy-duty mercerized cotton, cotton, synthetic thread	Denim	18/110
All weights: decorative topstitching	Silk or synthetic decorative thread	Topstitching	16/100
All weights: decorative hemming stitch, heirloom stitching	Medium mercerized cotton, synthetic thread, silk	Hemstitch, Microtex or sharp	18/110
Synthetic knits and stretch fabrics: polyester, double knit, jersey, panné velvet	Medium mercerized cotton, synthetic thread, silk	Ballpoint or stretch	14/90 11/75
Leather: suede, kidskin	Medium mercerized cotton, synthetic thread, silk	Leather	11/75 14/90 16/100
Light- and medium-weight fabrics: decorative multi-needle stitching	Medium mercerized cotton	Twin or triple	14/90
Medium-weight fabric: machine quilting	Medium cotton, synthetic thread, silk	Quilting or stippling	11/75 14/90
Medium-weight fabric: free-motion machine quilting	Medium cotton, synthetic thread, silk	Spring	14/90
Light- or medium-weight fabric: machine embroidery	Silk or synthetic decorative thread	Embroidery or spring	14/90 16/100

Spring needle: this needle has a wire spring above the point to prevent fabrics from riding up onto the needle, so eliminating the need for a presser foot. It is used in free-motion stitching with dropped feed dog. Before using, practice free-motion stitching on paper with a heavy universal needle and dropped feed dog. Don't pull the paper or fabric, but gently guide it through the stitching. Wear safety glasses for free-motion work, since needles quite often break.

Topstitching needle: specifically for topstitching, this needle has an extra-sharp point, extra-large eye, and a large groove for heavier thread. Use the smallest size needle that will accommodate your thread to avoid punching large holes in the fabric.

Twin or double needle: two needles on a single shaft to produce two rows of stitches and used for topstitching, pin tucking, and decorative stitching. Twin needles have a slightly different two-number sizing system; the first number on the package represents the distance between the two needles in millimeters (from 1.6mm to 6mm), and the second number indicates the needle size. Twin needles are available with universal, stretch, embroidery, denim, and Metallica points. A triple needle (2.5mm and 3mm widths) is also available.

Universal needle: this is the safest needle choice for most fabric types. It has a slightly rounded point and an elongated scarf, which helps the needle to meet the bobbin hook neatly. However, if the fabric is anything other than a medium-weight woven type, it will be better to use a needle specifically suited to it.

BOBBINS

The bobbin holds the lower thread and sits under the needle plate. Your sewing machine will probably come with one or two bobbins, but it is worth buying more so you can keep a stock of the thread colors you use most often already wound and ready to go.

BOBBIN TECHNIQUES

Bobbins can be top-loading or side/front loading.

Removing a top-loading bobbin
On top-loading machines the bobbin is taken out of the bobbin case for winding, so the bobbin case normally remains in the machine. The bobbin is accessed via a sliding or hinged panel in the needle plate in front of the needle. Raise the needle and lift the presser foot, then remove the plate and take the empty bobbin out of the machine.

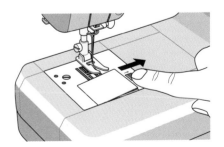

Removing a front-loading bobbin
On front-loading machines the whole bobbin case is taken out of the machine and then the bobbin is removed from the case for winding.

A1 The bobbin is accessed via a door at the front or side of the machine, below the needle. Raise the needle and lift the presser foot, then open the door.

A2 Take hold of the hinged latch on top of the bobbin and pull it towards you – the entire bobbin case with the bobbin inside should slide out of the machine. Still holding the latch, tip the empty bobbin out of the bobbin case.

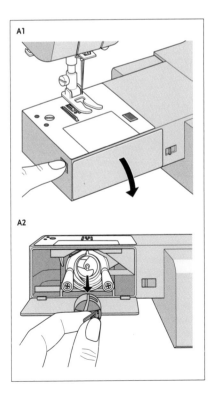

Winding the bobbin

On most machines the bobbin winding mechanism is on top of the machine on the right, but check your manual before you begin.

B1 Place a spool of thread on a spool pin and thread up for bobbin winding as indicated on the machine or in the manual. In general, the thread goes from the spool, through a single bobbin thread guide, then straight over towards the bobbin. Feed the end of the thread into the securing hole on the bobbin, if there is one, and hold the end in position. Take a couple of turns around the bobbin with some of the thread going back towards the spool until the thread is securely held in position on the bobbin. Place the bobbin on the bobbin winder spindle, making sure any springs or clips engage. The thread leading back to the spool should be reasonably taut – if necessary, tighten it by winding back the thread spool rather than by turning the bobbin.

B2 Engage the bobbin winding mechanism, either by moving the stitch selector to a bobbin winding position or by pushing the bobbin winder stopper over. Holding the loose end of thread on the bobbin, start the machine – the bobbin will spin and take on thread. Let go of the thread end as soon as there is enough thread on the bobbin to secure it. Don't try to guide the thread; it should automatically feed over the whole width of the bobbin. Do not overfill the bobbin. Many machines have a built-in device to stop winding when the bobbin is full. If your machine has such a device, wind until it cuts in and then remove the bobbin from the bobbin spindle.

> **TIP** The bobbin winding mechanism may incorporate a small blade that automatically cuts the thread when it reaches the correct level. If not, fill the bobbin no further than its edges.

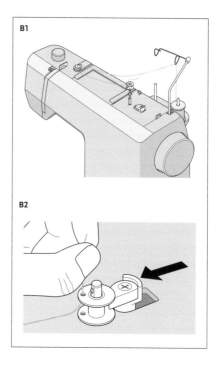

B1

B2

FAST BOBBIN WINDING

✂ If you can't find a bobbin winding spindle on top of your machine, check if it has an access door on the right-hand side or front of the casing that conceals the bobbin winding mechanism.

✂ You can buy stand-alone hand-held bobbin winding machines so you can fill bobbins without disturbing the threading or stitching function on the sewing machine at all.

✂ If you plan to buy a stand-alone bobbin winder, check that it will work with your machine's bobbins – most standard formats are accommodated, but unusual sizes may not wind evenly.

✂ The bobbin winding mechanism can always be identified by finding the short winding spindle, sometimes with a separate spool pin nearby.

✂ A bobbin storage box will keep wound bobbins neat and tidy so they are ready when you need them.

✂ To wind the bobbin without unthreading the needle, disengage the stitching mechanism so the needle does not go up and down as you wind. On some machines this happens automatically; on others you will need to disengage the stitching function manually by turning a knob on the hand wheel.

A stand-alone bobbin winder, like Simplicity's SideWinder™, can use a power cord or run on batteries so you can use it anywhere.

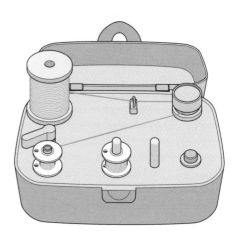

Replacing a top-loading bobbin

Simply put back into the bobbin case.

C1 Drop the wound bobbin into the bobbin case so the thread is coming off in a counterclockwise direction.

C2 Slide the thread into the notch on the front of the bobbin case and pull it left and back so it slides under the tension spring on the outside of the case.

C3 The thread should slide down to the base of the tension spring and come out through the second notch at the left side. Pull out 4in (10cm) of bobbin thread.

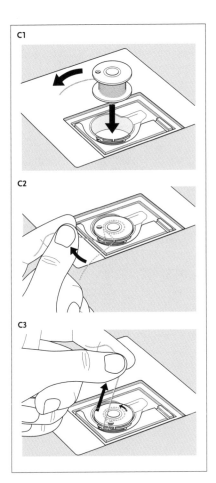

Replacing a front-loading bobbin

With a front-loading machine the bobbin is put back into the bobbin case and then the case is returned to the machine.

D1 Drop the wound bobbin into the bobbin case, making sure that the bobbin is the right way up so the thread is coming off in a clockwise direction.

D2 Slide the thread into the slot on the side of the bobbin case and pull it back under the tension spring on the outside of the bobbin case.

D3 The thread should slide right to the base of the tension spring and come out through the small eye at the bottom.

D4 Holding the bobbin case by the latch again, slide it back into the machine, aligning the protruding rib with the corresponding notch inside. Pull out and leave about 4in (10cm) of bobbin thread dangling loose.

CHECKING THE BOBBIN

✂ Pull gently on the bobbin thread before you start threading up the machine. If it pulls out of the bobbin very freely, the thread is not running through the tension spring correctly – you should be able to feel a slight resistance. Take the bobbin out and start again.

✂ Use only the correct bobbin for your machine as using the wrong bobbin may cause your machine to malfunction. If the machine came with plastic bobbins, do not use metal ones, and vice versa.

✂ Always use the correct bobbin from the manufacturer of your machine. There is no generic bobbin that will fit all machines.

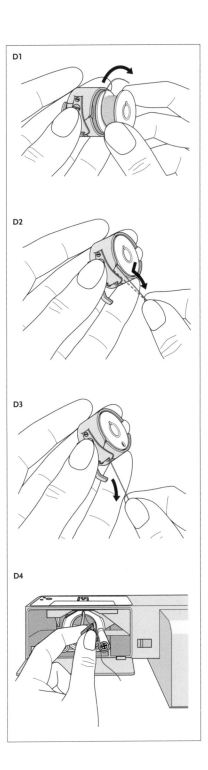

THREADING TECHNIQUES

Most machines thread in more or less the same way, with only a few minor variations. The thread must travel from the spool, through the thread take-up lever and the tension plates to the needle, via a variable number of thread guides along the way.

THREADING UP

Most machines must be threaded manually, although some computerized machines have an automatic threading system (for instructions on how to use this, consult the machine's manual).

Manual threading

A1 Raise the presser foot and raise the needle to its highest position, either by turning the hand wheel towards you or by pressing the up/down needle button. Place a spool of thread on the spool pin. Push on a spool holder to hold the spool in place if one is provided with the machine. Pull out a short length of thread.

A2 Take the end of the thread across the top of the machine to the first thread guide and insert the thread in the guide – it is usually shaped so you can just slide the thread in. There will be at least one guide, maybe two or even more, leading the thread from the spool towards the tension mechanism.

A3 Bring the thread down the front of the machine, through the tension mechanism. This is usually a pair of tension discs on the front of the machine with the tension dial on top. On some machines the discs are hidden inside a channel going down the front of the machine and the tension dial is set on top or to one side (inset). The thread needs to go between the two discs and

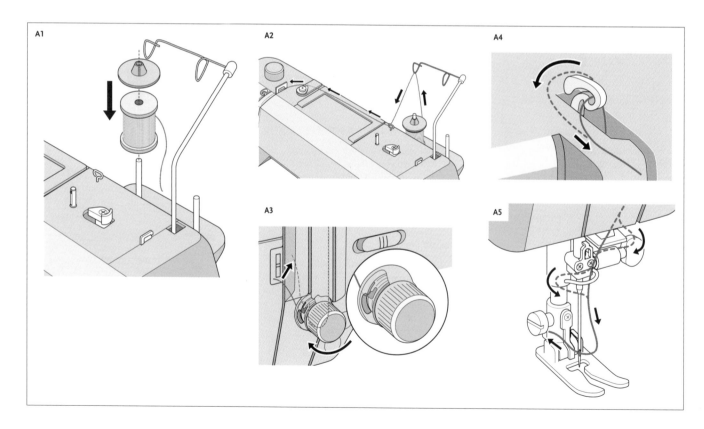

over the check spring; getting the thread correctly between these is crucial to achieve good stitching – give a little tug upwards to be sure it is firmly in place.

A4 From the tension mechanism, the thread needs to go to the take-up mechanism, which is the lever on the front of the machine that goes up and down when the needle is stitching. Take the thread through the take-up lever – usually it is shaped so you can slide the thread in, but you may have to thread it through a large eye.

A5 Now the thread needs to go back down the front of the machine on the left side of the take-up lever towards the needle. Slide it through the thread guide on the front of the machine at the bottom, and through the one just above the needle on the needle bar.

A6 Insert the thread through the eye of the needle, in the direction indicated in the manual – on most machines this will be from front to back. Pull the thread end through gently, leaving it long enough to pull to the back so it can be secured under the foot when you begin sewing.

THREADS FOR THE MACHINE

✂ There are many different thread brands and types, some general-purpose and some for specific tasks – buy the right type for your project (see fabric/needle chart on page 34).

✂ Use good-quality thread – cheap or old thread will break more easily, shedding lint that will build up and clog the machine.

✂ Threads marked for hand stitching may not be strong enough for machine use, although machine threads will be suitable for hand sewing too.

USING AN AUTO THREADER

Many modern machines have a semi-automatic needle threader, which can save time if you are a novice sewer or have poor eyesight. Different models may have slightly different systems, but the basic instructions are the same.

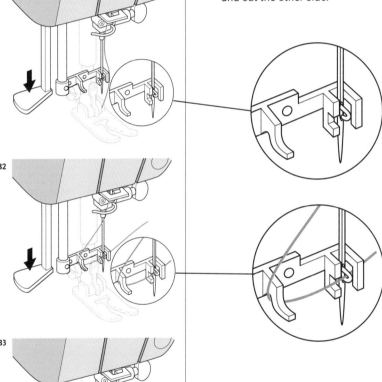

B1 Make sure the needle is at its highest point, either by turning the hand wheel or by pressing the up/down needle button. Press the needle threader handle with one finger; as it comes down a tiny hook will move around and through the needle eye.

B2 Take the thread to the needle and guide it under the plastic hook to the left of the threader, under the tiny hook coming through the eye of the needle, and out the other side.

B3 Slowly release the needle threader handle so it moves back to its resting position. The tiny hook will pull a loop of the thread through the eye as it goes. Catch the loop of thread from the back of the needle and pull the end through.

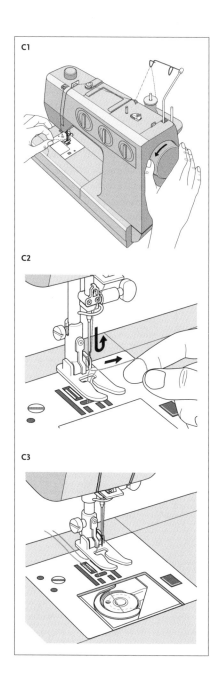

C1

C2

C3

Raising the bobbin thread

The final step in the threading process is to bring the end of the bobbin thread up through the needle plate.

C1 Make sure the needle and bobbin are threaded correctly, then take hold of the end of the needle thread and grip it firmly between finger and thumb. Turn the hand wheel once, or press the up/down needle button twice, so the needle goes down through the needle plate and back up again – don't let go of the thread end as this happens.

C2 The top thread will catch the bottom thread and pull a loop of it back up through the needle plate. Pull gently on the needle thread to raise the loop upwards until you can get hold of it.

C3 Take hold of the loop and pull gently to bring the loose end of the bobbin thread through to the top. On a top-loading bobbin model you can then check the bobbin – the thread should pass diagonally across the top of the bobbin. Take the needle thread under the presser foot and feed both thread ends to the back of the machine.

THREAD TENSION

Both the top (needle) thread and the bottom (bobbin) thread are held under tension as the machine stitches, and to achieve a perfect line of stitching the tension should be the same on both sides of the fabric. To achieve this the tension is usually adjusted on the top thread only, using a numbered dial. The tension on the bobbin thread can be adjusted in extreme cases by turning a screw in the bobbin case, but most manufacturers recommend leaving the bottom tension to the factory setting and altering it may invalidate the sewing machine's warranty.

> **TIP** If the thread keeps breaking, make sure your machine is correctly threaded – particularly through the tension plates – and that the spool is able to turn easily to release thread. Check the tension – you may have it set incorrectly for the fabric and thread you are using.

THREADING TIPS

✄ Many machines have a threading diagram noted somewhere on the machine, so even if you no longer have the manual you should have something to follow.

✄ The spool holder stops the spool jumping around too much on the pin as the thread unwinds. Don't push it down on top of the spool too firmly – the spool should still be able to turn on the pin freely.

✄ Make sure the thread goes between the tension discs and take-up lever correctly. Before threading the needle, check the machine is correctly threaded to this point.

✄ To check before needle threading, lower the presser foot and pull down on the thread just above the needle – it should resist; if it runs freely, rethread.

✄ Always thread the eye of the needle from the side that has the long groove (always on the opposite side to the flat section of the shank). On most machines you will be threading from front to back.

✄ Thread the top thread with the presser foot lifted and try to keep the thread reasonably taut. If there is slack thread anywhere when you have finished, take it up by turning the thread spool.

Checking the tension

To test the tension is correct, stitch a seam on a scrap of the fabric you will be using for your project.

EXAMPLE 1

If the tension is the same on both top and bottom threads, the stitch is perfectly balanced, so the two threads interlink in the middle of the layers of fabric. The line of stitching will look exactly the same on both sides.

EXAMPLE 2

If the bottom thread is tighter than the top thread, the bottom thread will lie in a line with loops of the top thread showing over the top. Tighten the top thread tension to correct this.

EXAMPLE 3

If the top thread is tighter than the bottom thread, the top thread will lie in a line with loops of the bottom thread showing over the top. Loosen the top thread tension to correct this.

Example 1: Balanced stitch.

Example 2: Top thread too loose.

Example 3: Top thread too tight.

Adjusting needle thread tension

You adjust the top thread tension by turning a dial on the front of the machine, near the tension plates. Normal tension for the specific model is usually highlighted on the dial in some way, so you can return to normal easily after adjusting the tension for special conditions.

Adjusting bobbin thread tension

You adjust the bottom thread tension by taking out the bobbin case and turning a small screw on the outside. **NOTE:** On some machines this may invalidate the warranty. Consider buying a spare bobbin case to adjust as necessary, keeping the original at factory settings.

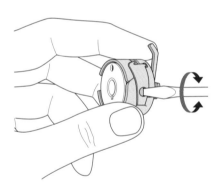

ADJUSTING STITCHES

You may want to alter the stitch length when you are sewing different fabrics, for a particular purpose – such as machine basting or gathering – or simply for decorative effect. The width of the stitch can also be altered, either to create zigzag stitching, to sew on buttons, or to change the needle drop position (see page 33).

Changing stitch length or width

Although the stitch length and width are usually selected before you start to stitch, they can also often be changed as you sew for extra decorative effects.

The stitch length is increased or decreased by turning the stitch length dial, sliding a lever backwards and forwards, or by selecting the stitch length icon and pressing on a + or – button. Longer-length stitches are used for machine basting, gathering, heavier fabrics and for decorative purposes. Shorter stitches are used for lightweight fabrics and for decoration. A mid-range size is best for most regular sewing.

The stitch width is increased or decreased by turning the stitch width dial, sliding a lever backwards and forwards, or by selecting the stitch width icon and pressing on a + or – button. For normal straight stitch the stitch width should be set at 0, but when stitching zigzag, increase as required to create a narrower or wider zigzag pattern.

When stitching zigzag, if you keep the width the same but decrease the stitch length, the zigzag stitching will close up to give a denser pattern. If you increase the stitch length, the zigzag stitching moves apart for a more open pattern.

TEST STITCHING

✂ If you experience problems, first check the needle – a damaged or blunt needle can lead to skipped stitches.

✂ If your stitching appears uneven, you may have threaded the machine with the presser foot down. Many machines must be threaded with the presser foot raised, to feed the thread through the tension plates correctly. Try rethreading.

SERGER ANATOMY

A serger stitches in a different way than a conventional sewing machine: it often has more than one needle and uses several loopers instead of one bobbin. This section covers the basic parts common to most sergers.

FRONT

1 Foot pressure dial: adjustable foot pressure allows you to sew very lightweight or heavyweight fabrics more successfully. This function may not be available on all models.

2 Differential feed dial: can be adjusted to prevent waving seams on stretch fabrics and to ensure pucker-free seams on lightweight fabrics. This function may not be available on all models (see Differential Feed, opposite).

3 Flat bed: with some sergers it is possible to remove part of the bed to create a free-arm facility just as it is on some conventional sewing machines.

4 Needle plate: some sergers come with a second needle plate for stitching rolled hems; others have a special plate already built in – you need to pull a lever or press a button to bring it into play.

5 Stitch or cutting width dial: to regulate the width of the serged seam.

6 Presser foot: holds the fabric against the needle plate and feed dog. Like a sewing machine, the serger has different types of foot for different tasks, but serger and sewing machine feet are not interchangeable.

7 Needle: sergers may have one, two or three needles; use the recommended needle for your machine. Serger and sewing machine needles are not generally interchangeable.

8 Hinged case: the lower section of the body opens up to access the threading areas for the loopers. There is often a color-coded threading diagram inside.

9 Stitch patterns: illustrated reference for the types of stitch that can be sewn, with reference numbers that match those on the stitch selector.

10 Needle clamp screws: to release the needles when they require changing.

11 Looper thread tension levers: used to adjust the tension of the looper threads; there may be two or three, depending on the model. The loopers are located in the interior of the serger, accessed by a hinged door – they create the knitted look of the serger seam.

12 Needle thread tension levers: used to adjust the tension of the upper needle threads; there may be one, two or three, depending on the model.

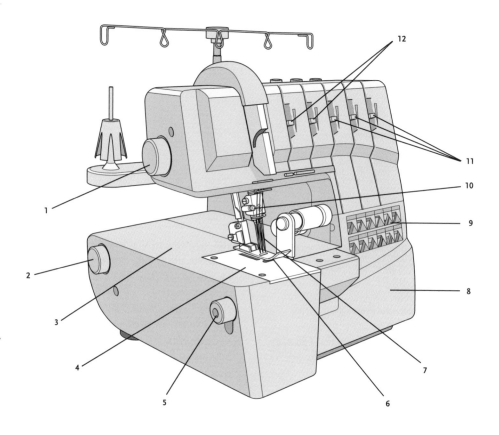

BACK

13 Thread guide: each separate thread has its own guide. The threading runs are color-coded for ease of threading.

14 Stitch selector dial: for selecting the type of serger stitch to be sewn.

15 Stitch length dial: for regulating the length of the stitches.

16 Hand wheel: turn the hand wheel towards you (counterclockwise) to move the needle up and down slowly or to take the new thread through when rethreading using the knot method.

17 Power switch: to turn the machine on and off.

18 Power socket: socket for the power cable and the foot pedal; on some models there may be a separate socket for the foot pedal.

19 Telescopic rod: can be extended to take the thread guide hanger up to its full height or telescoped down for easier storage.

20 Presser foot lifting lever: this is behind the thread spool and is used to lift the presser foot to slide the fabric beneath, or when changing the foot.

21 Thread spool pins: hold the thread for the needles and the loopers, one for each threading run. Sergers use a great deal of thread, so larger spools or cones are a better option.

22 Thread guide hanger: each thread guide should be positioned above a corresponding cone beneath. Make sure the thread guide hanger is pulled up to its full height on its telescopic rod.

Cutting blades (not shown): a serger has a lower blade and an upper blade, which can be retracted if you want to stitch without trimming the fabric edge.

Differential feed

Differential feed is a variation of drop feed with two independent sets of feed dog, one before and one after the needle. By changing their relative motions, these sets of feed dog can be used to stretch or compress the material near the needle. This is very useful when sewing stretchy fabrics or for creating special effects, such as a lettuce edge (see page 62). Differential feed is not found on sewing machines, although the dual feed or walking foot covers some of its functions, so it is worth considering a serger if you plan to work with stretchy fabrics often.

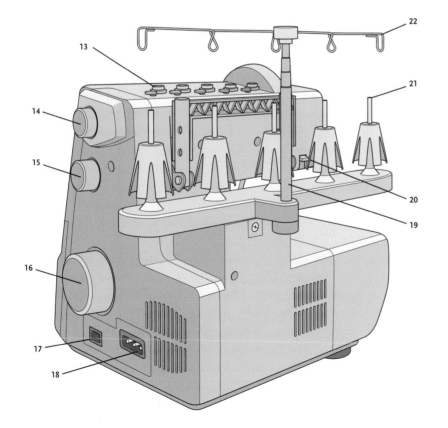

> **TIP** There will be variations depending on make and model, and on how many threads the serger accommodates. Different models may have different controls in alternative positions, so take time to study your machine's manual.

THREADING A SERGER

Since a serger uses between two and five spools of thread and has no bobbin, it is threaded in a different way than a conventional sewing machine. The basic principles are shown here.

MODEL VARIATION

Do make sure you follow the exact order of threading given in your machine's manual, which can vary from model to model, or you may find the thread keeps breaking when you try to stitch. Many people don't consider a serger because they are afraid it will be too difficult to thread, but once you understand the principles of how the machine works you will soon find threading quite easy.

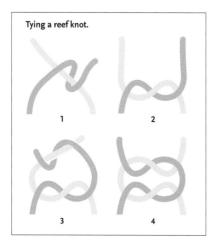

Tying a reef knot.

1 2
3 4

Threading up using the knot method

The easiest way to thread a serger with existing threads in place is to knot the new thread to an existing thread and pull the new thread through, either by winding the hand wheel or pulling through by hand.

Tie the new thread to the end of the old using a flat reef knot. To tie a reef knot, take the ends of thread, one in each hand. Take the left end over the right end and under, so the left end is now on the right and vice versa. Take the end now on the right over the one on the left and under. You should now have a symmetrical flat knot. Trim the thread ends, but not too close to the knot as it may pull undone.

Make sure the presser foot lever is up and loosen the tension dials to 0, then wind the new threads through the serger using the hand wheel, or pull each through gently one at a time from above the needle or looper eye. Ease the knot gently at key points – such as through the tension plates. On the needle threads, stop the knot before the eye of the needle, snip it off and thread the needle by hand. If not done automatically, reset the tension when the machine is correctly rethreaded.

On the diagram below the two needles are threaded in red and blue, the upper looper in yellow, the lower looper in orange and the chain-stitch looper in green.

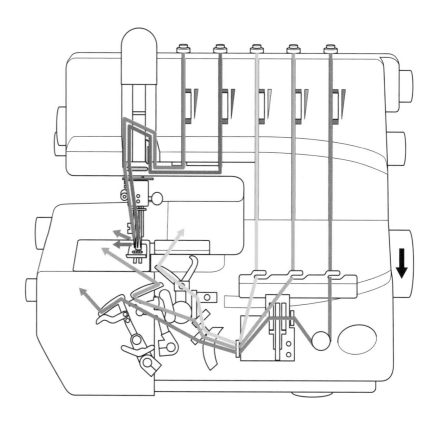

Threading from scratch

If the thread has completely run out on one or more of the runs, you will need to thread up from scratch. Early sergers were quite complex to thread, but modern types are much easier and some even have a self-threading mechanism. Sergers must be threaded in a certain order because of the way the threads pass across one another. If you thread them in the wrong order, as you move the hand wheel to access the threading runs the needle threads can get tangled around the looper threads, and these will break when you begin to stitch. Check your manual to be sure of the correct threading order.

To thread the first looper: take the thread from the spool, up through the corresponding eye on the thread hanger and down to its matching thread guide on top of the machine. Slide the thread through the tension mechanism and then into the thread guide directly below the tension dial or lever. Slip the thread into the next guides in order along the threading run, which is usually indicated by color-coded dots or a colored line. Take the thread through the eye of the looper, then pull the end towards the back of the serger, leaving around 6in (15cm) hanging free. Repeat for the other loopers, following the corresponding color-coded runs.

To thread the first needle: take the thread from the spool, up through the corresponding eye on the thread hanger and down to its matching thread guide on top of the machine. Slide the thread through the tension mechanism and then into the thread guide directly below the tension dial or lever. Take it under the guide to the left then over the top thread path, following the color-coded thread run. Take the thread through the wire guide at the top of the needle and then through the eye of the needle. Pull the end towards the back of the serger, under the foot, leaving around 6in (15cm) hanging free. Repeat for the other needle or needles, following the corresponding color-coded runs.

AVOIDING THREADING PROBLEMS

✂ If you have just purchased a new machine it may have threads in place running through the machine with the ends hanging from the loops on the thread guide hanger towards the spool pins. Do not remove, as they are there to help you to thread the machine the first time. Use the knot method (see opposite page).

✂ Never set the machine stitching to work the knots through, as they can easily damage the mechanism.

✂ If threading from scratch, the loopers should always be threaded before the needles. Some sergers are best threaded in the following order: lower looper; upper looper; right needle; left needle. On others the order is: upper looper; lower looper; right needle; left needle. Check your machine's manual.

✂ If the looper thread breaks, you will have to unthread the needle threads from the eye of the needle before trying to rethread the looper.

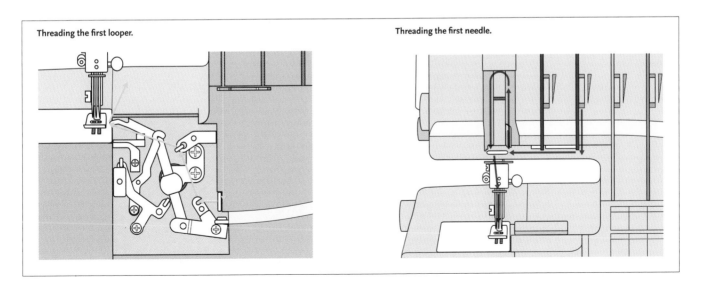

Threading the first looper.

Threading the first needle.

THREAD TENSION

Each thread on a serger has its own tension control and changing the tension on one will affect how the threads loop together and so how the final stitch will look. It's a useful exercise to sew some practice seams with a different color thread in each thread run. This will show you where each thread goes and the effect caused by adjusting the tension on different needles or loopers.

Checking the tension

To test the tension is correct, stitch a seam on a scrap of the fabric you will be using for your project. On the following examples, the stitch has been created with three threads for clarity, but the principles are the same with more threads. The upper looper is threaded with yellow, the lower looper with orange, and the needle with red.

EXAMPLE 1

If the tension is correct, the looper threads (yellow upper and orange lower) form a smooth chain and interlock neatly at the raw edge. The needle thread (stitching in red) creates a flat even line of stitching on the top side of the fabric.

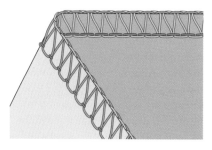

EXAMPLE 2

If the upper looper is too loose, the lower looper thread will pull it round to the underside of the fabric. Tighten the upper looper tension to correct this. In some cases this problem might be due to the lower looper thread being too tight; check the thread run to make sure the lower looper thread isn't caught anywhere.

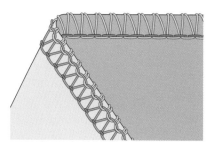

EXAMPLE 3

If the lower looper is too loose, the upper looper thread will pull it round to the top side of the fabric. Tighten the lower looper tension to correct this. In some cases this problem might be due to the upper looper thread being too tight; check the thread run to make sure the upper looper thread isn't caught anywhere.

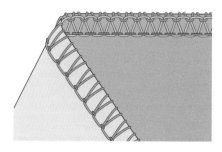

EXAMPLE 4

If both the lower and upper loopers are too tight, the fabric will be pulled into a roll at the raw edge instead of lying flat. Loosen the upper and the lower looper tension to correct this. Alternatively, the cutting width may need to be adjusted to remove more fabric.

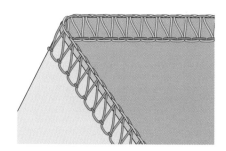

EXAMPLE 5
If both the lower and upper loopers are too loose, they will form loose loops over the edge instead of interlocking snugly. Tighten the upper and the lower looper tension to correct this. Alternatively, the cutting width may need to be adjusted to remove less fabric.

EXAMPLE 7
If the needle thread is too loose, the stitches will form loops on the underside of the fabric. Tighten the needle tension to correct this. (If there is more than one needle thread, adjust each individually.)

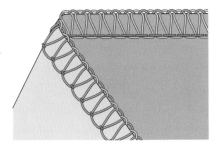

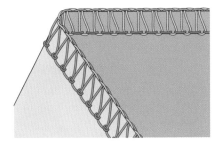

EXAMPLE 6
If the needle thread is too tight, the stitches will pucker the fabric and the seam will not lie flat. Loosen the needle tension to correct this. (If there is more than one needle thread, adjust each individually until the stitching lies flat.)

If you have a stitch problem that appears to be due to the tension but just can't be resolved by adjusting the tension, check the stitch width setting and the position of the cutting knife.

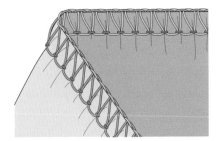

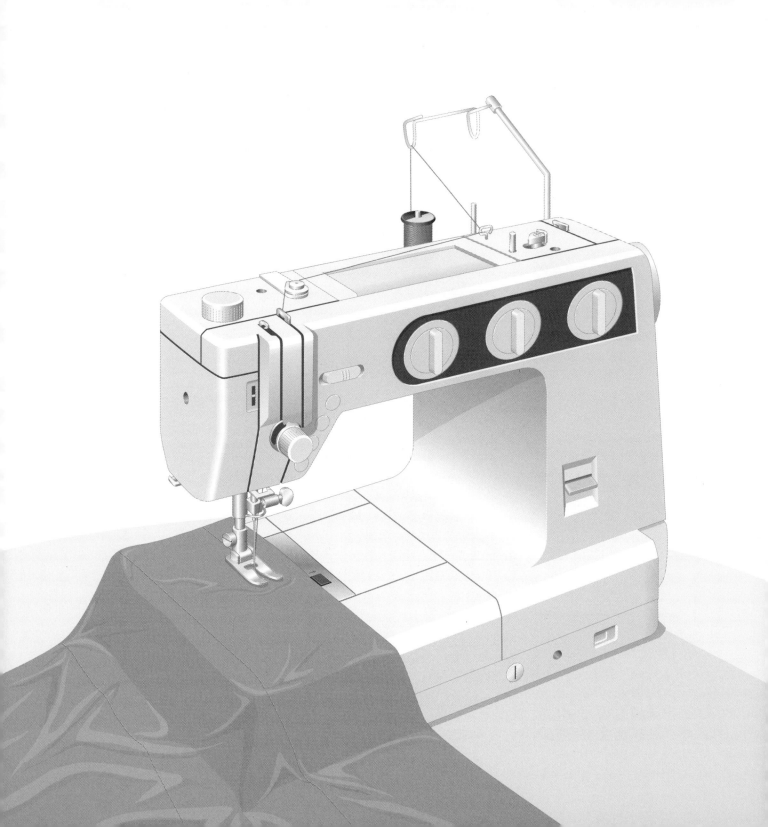

USING YOUR MACHINE

The time has come to get started with your sewing machine. The first few techniques covered here are the real basics of machine stitching. You will need to master these before moving on to the specific machine sewing techniques that are covered in the rest of this book. Practice sewing on easy-to-sew muslin (calico), and then explore working on more specialist fabrics. And, before turning to the technique chapters, take the chance to brush up on some sewing basics.

GETTING STARTED

You will get the best out of your machine if you are comfortable while using it. Make sure that you are sitting properly and that you are working in a good light (see page 24). Plug in the power cord, switch it on and you are ready to begin.

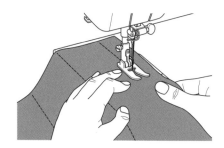

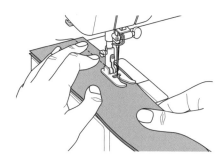

MACHINE STITCHING TECHNIQUES

If you are new to sewing with a machine, spend some time getting used to stitching with it before beginning work on a project.

Starting stitching
Make sure the needle and bobbin threads are pulled under and behind, or to the side, of the raised presser foot. Place the fabric under the presser foot so that the bulk of the fabric is to the left of the presser foot. Turn the hand wheel or press the needle down button to lower the needle into the fabric. Lower the presser foot and begin stitching, starting off slowly.

Where to position your hands
As you continue to stitch, your hands should be positioned on either side of the needle so that you can guide the fabric through the machine easily.

Controlling the pace
On an electric machine the foot pedal or the knee bar controls the speed at which you stitch. The harder you push, the faster the machine will go. Push it slowly at first, just enough to get the machine going. Many modern machines also have a speed control, usually a separate slider, which can be set to limit the maximum sewing speed.

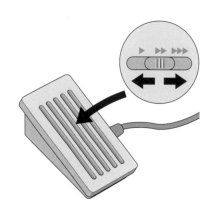

Guiding the fabric through the machine
Keep the bulk of the material to the left of the needle. Use your hands to steer the fabric in the right direction and to keep the edge aligned with the seam allowance guide (see below). Don't pull or push the fabric to move it through the machine – let the feed dog move it at the correct pace to match the action of the needle.

Using the seam allowance guide
To keep seam allowances even, look for lines on the needle plate that indicate common seam allowances – the space between the edge of the fabric and the stitching line. In most cases the seam allowance will be ⅝in (15mm), ½in (12mm), or ¼in (6mm). If you want to use an unusual seam allowance width, you can mark it yourself with masking tape.

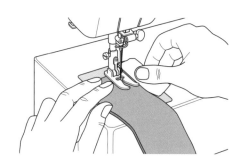

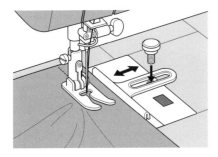

Using a magnetic or screw-on guide

A magnetic or screw-on cloth guide is designed to attach to the needle plate and can be adjusted to the correct distance from the needle. At the start of stitching, the edge of the fabric is aligned with the guide.

Securing the thread ends

Backstitch, the reverse stitch on the sewing machine, is used to reinforce the stitching at the beginning and end of a seam to prevent the threads pulling loose. Start off around ½in (12mm) from the beginning of the seam and reverse stitch back to the edge, then stitch forward as normal. At the end, finish by reversing back along the stitching line for around ½in (12mm).

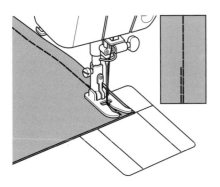

✂ Keep your fingers clear of the needle while sewing.

✂ Don't pull or push the fabric through the machine as you sew – this can bend the needle and may cause it to hit the needle plate and break. Let the feed dog do the work – your hands should just be guiding the fabric into the machine and keeping it straight.

✂ If the needle does not want to go into the fabric, you may be trying to sew through too much thickness. Try using a needle designed for a heavyweight fabric (see the fabric/needle chart on page 34). It's also possible that your machine is not heavy-duty enough to handle multiple layers of very thick fabric, although you might be able to stitch over a small area by using the hand wheel to ease the needle in and out.

✂ Try to avoid sewing with an almost empty bobbin or spool of thread – the thread may not feed evenly, which will cause stitching problems.

✂ It will take practice to stitch at a steady speed while steering the material under the needle. If your machine has a speed limiter function, it can help you to control your pace as you get to grips with the machine stitching technique.

✂ Don't spend too long working in one position – get up and walk around to stretch your muscles and avoid eyestrain.

✂ Good-quality stitching is dependent on having the correct needle, thread, tension and stitch length for the fabric you are using. Always test-stitch on a scrap of the actual fabric before you begin any major project.

Turning a corner

Follow these simple steps to achieve a neat, sharp turn in a seam when it needs to go around a corner.
A1 Stitch to the exact point at which you need to turn. Leaving the needle down in the fabric, lift the presser foot.
A2 Swivel the work around on the needle – being careful not to pull on the needle – so that you are stitching in the new direction. Lower the presser foot, then begin stitching again.

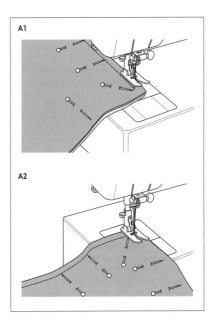

STITCH GLOSSARY

These are your basic machine stitches. Take the time to practice them on different weights and types of fabric before starting work on a specific project. For more on fabric types, see pages 53–55.

Straight stitch

This is the most basic type of machine stitching possible. For most straight stitching on seams, the stitch length on the machine should be set at around 2–3. When using straight stitching for decorative stitching, try out the stitch length on a scrap of the actual fabric you will be using to select the best stitch length for the effect you want to achieve.

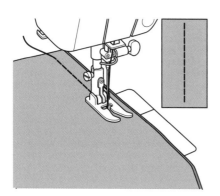

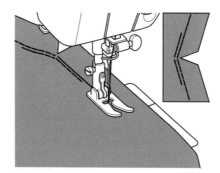

Staystitching

A single or double line of straight stitching through only a single thickness of fabric and within the seam allowance, so when the seam is stitched it will not be seen on the outside. It is used to hold stretch fabrics or curved lines, such as a neckline, in their original shape and prevent them from stretching under construction.

Easestitching

Easestitching is used to reduce the length of an edge so it can be joined to a slightly shorter edge without visible folds or gathers. Stitch a single line between the points to be eased with the stitch length at its longest setting. Pin the two edges together at the ends, then pull the bobbin thread on the stitching to distribute the fullness of the edge evenly. Stitch the seam with the eased edge on top and the flat edge below.

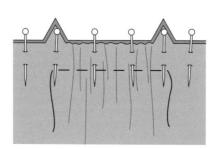

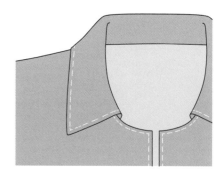

Edgestitching

A line of stitching made approximately ⅛in (3mm) from a seamline or fold line or very close to a finished edge to keep the edge crisp. It is usually done in thread to match the fabric.

Topstitching

An extra line of stitching made parallel to a finished edge, topstitching is usually done in contrasting thread as a decorative feature. It may also be used to attach items such as patch pockets or to keep seam allowances flat. To make topstitching more pronounced, slightly loosen the top thread tension. If the stitching is being done through several layers, it may also be necessary to adjust the foot pressure.

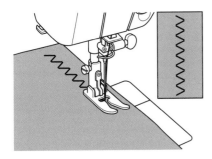

Zigzag

Zigzag stitch is used to finish raw edges and to stitch seams that need to have some give, such as for knit fabrics. The stitch width controls the width of the line of zigzag; the stitch length controls how tightly together the stitches are.

Twin needle sewing

The twin needle unit consists of two separate needles mounted on a crossbar, with a single shaft that fits into the needle clamp. Two threads are threaded through the machine together. At the final thread guide they run down on opposite sides, one to each needle.

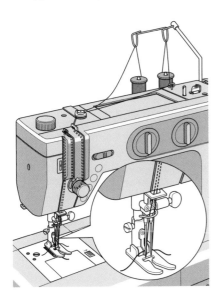

STITCHING FABRICS

It is one thing to practice machine stitching on muslin (calico) but quite another when you come to work on other fabrics, as you will when you begin using your sewing machine to make your own projects. It helps to understand a little about fabric structure and the challenges of working with certain fabrics before you begin.

FABRIC STRUCTURE

Fabric can be woven, knitted or nonwoven and each type has different characteristics, strengths and weaknesses.

Woven fabrics

All woven fabrics are made up of two sets of yarn – the warp and the weft. The warp runs lengthwise in the loom and is sometimes also known as the floating yarn/threads. The weft runs widthwise at right angles to the warp and is sometimes known as the filling yarn, the filler or the woof. Woven fabrics can be created with different patterns by using warp and weft yarns in different sequences.

The selvage is the border that runs lengthwise down both edges of a length of woven fabric. Since it is often woven more tightly than the main fabric to stop the edges fraying the selvage may pucker when the fabric is cleaned, so generally it is cut away and discarded for sewing projects. The lengthwise and widthwise direction – or grain – of a woven fabric is firm, so fabric has very little give in these directions. However, if pulled diagonally – or on the bias – the fabric will stretch. True bias is at a 45-degree angle to the selvage. Edges cut on the bias tend to stretch out of shape easily so seams must be stitched with care. In dressmaking, however, fabric is often cut and stitched on the bias as it results in clothes that drape and move with the body.

Knitted fabrics

All knitted fabrics are constructed using one set of yarn running in the same direction – looping the yarn around itself holds knit fabrics together. Some knits have their yarn running along the length of the fabric, others have their yarn running across the width. The columns of stitches that run the length of a knitted fabric are called wales, and the stitches running across form rows. Because of its construction, knitted fabric has some give in every direction, so it is ideal for form-fitting garments, but is less often used for furnishings. Most knits will need to be overstitched or serged to finish the edges and prevent unraveling.

Nonwoven fabrics

This category includes fabrics such as felt, interfacing, lace and net. Interfacing is a compressed synthetic fabric used as

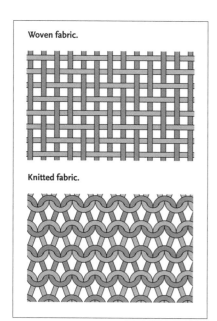

Woven fabric.

Knitted fabric.

a backing to the main project fabric, particularly in dressmaking and tailoring, to give extra body, shaping and support. Lace and net are made of yarns that are knotted into intricate patterns, and can either be machine- or handmade.

FABRIC COMPOSITION

Natural fibers include cotton, wool, linen and silk. Synthetic fibers include polyester, nylon, acrylic and rayon. Some fabrics and threads are made from more than one natural fiber or from natural and synthetic fibers mixed together in various percentages – such as polycotton, which is a mix of polyester and cotton. This mixing of fibers is often to improve the qualities of the original fiber – to make it more hardwearing, easier to wash, less prone to creasing or to create a better drape.

Pure cotton is the ideal sewing material, because it feels good to handle, drapes well, washes without any problems and presses easily. It is available in a wide range of colors and patterns, and in many different weaves and textures.

Many modern synthetics or natural/synthetic mixes are very easy to work with too. However, one of the joys of doing your own sewing is the chance to use unusual fabrics. Although these fabrics will require some extra time and attention, if you follow the tips given here you should still achieve professional-looking results.

Silk

The most beautiful items can be made of silk – the play of light and shade can bring a whole new dimension to the design. Silk is available in many weights and textures and in every color of the rainbow, and it is easy to press and pleasing to work. However, it is very slippery and frays easily. Use very fine pins and try to keep all pinning within the seam allowance because silk will retain pin marks. Cut silk on top of a cotton sheet to stop it sliding around too much, and use very sharp scissors. Hand baste all but the simplest seams. Sheer silks will need a narrow French seam, but otherwise use a seam with as little bulk as possible.

Velvet, velveteen and corduroy

Pile fabrics have a nap – the short fibers have been brushed in one direction, or have raised threads or loops on the surface that are created in the weaving process. Depending on which way the light falls on these fabrics, or in which direction they are smoothed, they will look lighter or darker. The nap or pile should run in the same direction on each part of a garment or home décor project when in use, otherwise it will look as if it has been made with two different colors of fabric. Use fine pins to avoid marking the pile. When cutting, keep the fabric pile-side up and if you need to place a pattern edge on a fold, fold the fabric with the pile on the outside. When stitching, stitch with the direction of the pile and use a plain seam pressed open. Finish the edges of the seam in some way (see pages 78–79 for some options) because these fabrics tend to fray badly.

SEWING ON DIFFERENT FABRICS

✂ When you first get your machine, experiment with its functions on many different fabric types.

✂ The fabric thickness and weight will affect needle choice, tension and stitch length. Your sewing machine manual may provide guidance.

✂ When buying fabric for a new project, check its recommended usage – this is often given in the specification on a tag or the bolt end.

✂ Always test the machine on the fabric you will be using for the project before you begin work in earnest.

✂ Choose the right fabric for the job. Dressmaking fabrics, for example, will not generally be strong enough for the wear and tear suffered by upholstery. Upholstery fabric, on the other hand, may be sturdy but it will not drape well enough to be suitable for making window treatments or clothing.

Lace

Choose a simple style because too many seams will break up the lace design. Some lace designs are directional, so you will need to follow the same rules as for fabric with a nap. Use sharp pins and when placing pattern pieces on a fold, fold the fabric with the right side on the outside. If you need to match the design across a seam, use basting tape (see page 71). Since lace is generally quite open in design most items will require a lining, or you can mount the lace on an opaque backing fabric before beginning construction so that it is self-lined. If seam edges will show through, bind them as described on page 78.

Leather and suede

The maximum size of a piece of leather or suede is limited to the size of the original animal. Some areas of skin will be thinner than others, so when planning out a project avoid letting these fall where they will be subject to strain. Place all pattern pieces in the same direction and use only pins within the seam allowance – or you can use paperclips instead.

Do all fitting and pattern checking in a fabric toile first because once the leather or suede has been stitched the holes made by the needle are permanent. When sewing animal skins, use a wedge-pointed leather needle – its tip will pierce the surface cleanly.

When stitching round corners, make the corner blunt rather than very pointed. When seams are finished, stick the seam allowances down with a liquid adhesive suitable for leather. For an invisible finish at the hem you can turn the edge under and stick it in place with no stitching at all.

Stretch fabric

When pinning, use very fine pins and place them at right angles to the edge. When cutting, try not to stretch the edge out of shape. It is best to hand baste seams before machine stitching because this will help to keep the layers aligned as you stitch the seam. Snip through a basting stitch every 4in (10cm) or so; this will allow you to stretch the fabric slightly by holding it both in front and behind the presser foot as you stitch to keep it under tension. Stretching as you stitch helps to keep the stitching fairly loose so the thread will not break under strain when the seam stretches in use.

A serger is ideal to stitch seams in all types of stretch fabric. When sewing knitted fabrics, use a ballpoint needle, as the rounded tip will tend to slide between the yarn threads rather than piercing them.

BUYING FABRIC AND THREAD

✂ Note the composition of the fabric when you buy it and keep a record of any washing instructions.

✂ Check the fabric width with a tape measure before buying if it is critical to your project – imperial/metric conversions are not always exact and some speciality fabrics may come in unusual widths.

✂ If you are using patterned fabric or fabric with a pile or nap, you will need to allow for extra fabric for pattern matching and to ensure the pile or nap is running the same way.

✂ Buy thread at the same time that you buy your fabric. Since thread appears darker on the spool, lay a strand on the fabric to check you have the right color.

STANDARD FABRIC WIDTHS

Fabrics are available in standard widths, which may vary for different fabric types or on where it was woven. For instance, printed cotton for dressmaking was traditionally woven in inches and was either 36in (now usually labeled 90cm), 45in (now 112cm) or 54in (now 135cm) wide. Standard voile for drapes is wider, often 120in (now 300cm) wide, while pure silk may be only 18in (now 45cm) wide. If a manufacturer is still using an imperial loom, the metric fabric width may not be an exact conversion; a fabric woven on a 54-inch loom may be labeled 135cm wide but will actually be slightly wider (see table below). The conversion from imperial to metric has also meant that some standards have been changed – a fabric woven on a 54-inch loom will actually be 137cm wide, but the equivalent metric loom produces 140cm (55in) wide fabric. In most cases this slight variation will make no difference when the fabric is cut up to sew, but if the starting width of the fabric is critical, measure it yourself before purchasing.

OLD IMPERIAL WIDTH	NEW METRIC WIDTH
18in (45.7cm)	45cm
36in (91.4cm)	90cm
45in (114.3cm)	112cm
46in (116.8cm)	115cm
54in (137.1cm)	135cm
55in (139.7cm)	140cm
60in (152.4cm)	150cm
120in (304.8cm)	300cm

TROUBLE-SHOOTING

If something looks wrong with your stitching, or your machine appears to be malfunctioning, the problem is often very easy and simple to put right.

STITCHING PROBLEMS

PROBLEM	POSSIBLE CAUSE	SOLUTION
Irregular stitches	The top thread tension is too loose.	Tighten the top thread tension (see page 41).
	The fabric is being pulled manually through the machine faster than it can stitch.	Do not pull on the fabric – just guide it gently in the right direction, allowing the feed dog to do the work.
	The presser foot pressure is set too light.	Increase the pressure on the presser foot (see page 31).
	The presser foot is too loose.	Tighten or reset the presser foot (page 30).
Skipped stitches	The needle is bent, blunt or incorrectly inserted.	Change the needle. Make sure the needle is the correct way round (see page 32) and is fully inserted into the needle clamp.
	The needle and thread are not the correct type for the fabric being sewn.	Change the needle to the correct size and type for the fabric (see page 34) and use the correct thread.
	The top thread tension is too tight.	Reset the thread tension (see page 41).
	The thread take-up lever has not been threaded.	Rethread the machine correctly (see page 38), checking that the thread goes through the take-up lever.

PROBLEM	POSSIBLE CAUSE	SOLUTION
Stitches not formed properly	The thread has not been pulled into the thread tension unit.	Rethread the top thread correctly (see page 38), making sure that the presser foot is up, which opens up the tension mechanism to allow the thread to locate correctly, and that the thread is kept taut while threading.
	The bobbin case is incorrectly threaded.	Rethread the bobbin case correctly (page 37).
	The spool cap is the wrong size for the thread spool.	Replace the spool cap with the correct size.
Seams puckering	The top thread tension is too tight.	Reset the thread tension (see page 41).
	The top thread is not threaded correctly.	Rethread the top thread correctly, making sure that the presser foot is up and that the thread is kept taut while threading.
	The point of the needle is blunt or it is too heavy for the fabric being sewn.	Change the needle, making sure it is the correct size and type for the fabric being sewn (see page 34).
	The stitch length is too long for the fabric being sewn.	Decrease the stitch length (see page 41).
	The wrong presser foot is fitted.	Change the presser foot to the correct type.
	The fabric is too sheer or soft.	Layer the fabric with material backing or tissue paper before stitching the seam.
	There are two different sizes or kinds of thread in the machine.	Make sure the top thread and the bobbin thread are the same weight and type.
Thread looping/bunching under the fabric	The top thread tension is too loose.	Reset the thread tension (see page 41).
	The machine is not correctly threaded.	Rethread the top thread correctly, making sure that the presser foot is up and that the thread is kept taut while threading.
	The needle is not the correct type for the thread being used.	Change the needle to the correct size and type for the thread and fabric (see page 34) and use the correct thread.

PROBLEM	POSSIBLE CAUSE	SOLUTION
Fabric not feeding smoothly through the machine	The stitch length is set to 0.	Select the correct stitch length for the type of stitching.
	The feed dog is lowered.	Raise the feed dog (see page 31).
	Lint is caught under the needle plate.	Clean the machine (see page 25), particularly between the feed dog teeth.
	The stitch length is too short for the fabric being sewn.	Increase the stitch length (see page 41).
	The presser foot pressure is too low.	Set the presser foot pressure adjustment lever to normal (see page 31).
	The machine is set in buttonhole mode.	Select the correct stitch type and length.

OPERATIONAL PROBLEMS

PROBLEM	POSSIBLE CAUSE	SOLUTION
Needle breaks	The needle has not been fully or properly inserted into the needle clamp.	Make sure the needle is the correct way round (see page 32) and is fully inserted into the needle clamp.
	The needle clamp screw is loose.	Tighten the needle clamp screw securely.
	A too-fine needle was used for sewing a heavyweight material.	Change the needle to the correct size and type (see page 34) for the fabric being sewn.
	An incorrect presser foot is being used so the needle is catching on it.	Change to the correct presser foot for the type of stitching being done (see page 28).
	The presser foot is loose so the needle is catching it.	Tighten or replace the presser foot.
	The fabric is being pulled manually through the machine so the needle is being bent.	Do not pull on the fabric while stitching; just guide it gently in the right direction and let the feed dog do the work.

PROBLEM	POSSIBLE CAUSE	SOLUTION
Upper thread keeps breaking	The top threading is not correct or the tension is too tight.	Rethread the top thread correctly (see page 38), making sure that the presser foot is up, which opens up the tension mechanism to allow the thread to locate correctly, and that the thread is kept taut while threading.
	The needle is bent or blunt, is the wrong size or has been inserted incorrectly.	Change the needle, using the correct size and type for the fabric being stitched. Make sure the needle is the right way round (see page 32) and is fully inserted into the needle clamp.
	The thread is too heavy or fine for the needle being used.	Use quality thread and the correct needle (see page 34).
	The threads have not been drawn to the rear and secured under the presser foot before stitching is begun.	Pull the threads to the rear (see page 40) before beginning to sew.
	The machine is stitching too fast when starting off.	Start stitching at a medium/slow speed (see page 50).
	The thread has a knot in it or is of poor quality.	Check for and remove any knots; always use good-quality thread.
Bobbin thread keeps breaking	The bobbin has not been fully inserted in the bobbin case or is not correctly threaded.	Remove the bobbin, reinsert it into the bobbin case correctly, and rethread (see page 37).
	Lint has built up in the bobbin case or hook race.	Clean the machine (see page 25).
	The bobbin does not turn smoothly in the bobbin case.	Check to see that the bobbin has been wound evenly, is the right type and is not damaged.
Needle pushes the fabric down through the needle plate	The needle is blunt or the wrong size.	Change the needle, using the correct size and type (see page 34) for the fabric being stitched.

PROBLEM	POSSIBLE CAUSE	SOLUTION
The machine is not operating	No power is reaching the machine.	Make sure the foot control is pushed firmly into the machine socket, and the machine is plugged in and switched on. Check the fuse.
	The light bulb has blown; some machines don't work at all if the bulb has gone.	Replace the bulb.
	Thread is caught in the hook race, causing it to lock.	Clean the hook race and remove all loose threads (see page 25).
	The bobbin winder mechanism has been left in the winding position.	Put the bobbin winder mechanism back to the stitching position.
	The hand wheel is out of gear.	Check position and tightness of hand wheel.
	The buttonhole lever was not lowered when the machine was placed in buttonhole mode.	Lower the buttonhole lever.
No light, but machine still stitches	Blown bulb or light switch is not on.	Replace the bulb (see page 24) and make sure the light switch is on.
Machine suddenly stops while stitching	Thread is caught in the hook race, causing it to lock.	Clean the hook race and remove all loose threads (see page 25).
	The motor belt is slipping.	Send the machine for service.
Odd noise/machine jamming	Lint has accumulated in the feed dog or hook race.	Clean the machine (see page 25).
	A pin is caught in the machine.	Clean the machine (see page 25).
	Thread is caught in the hook race, causing it to lock.	Clean the hook race (see page 25).
Auto needle threader not working	The needle threader hook is bent or damaged.	Replace the needle threader hook.
	Needle is not at its highest position.	Turn the hand wheel until the needle reaches its highest position.
	Needle eye is not aligning with the threader hook.	Replace the needle (see page 32).

GETTING STARTED WITH THE SERGER

The serger is designed to stitch very fast and to cut the fabric as it stitches, so it has sharp, moving cutting blades. You need to be very aware of safety when you are using it, particularly when you are guiding the fabric towards the needle.

TIP A serger stitches with two, three, four or five threads, using different combinations of needles and loopers. A machine with the capability to handle more threads can be set up to use less, so will be more versatile.

SERGER TECHNIQUES

There are a few techniques that will help you to get the best from your serger.

Where to position your hands
As you stitch, it is important to keep your hands safely away from the cutting blade which is to the right of the presser foot. Place your left hand forward to move the fabric, and to guide and steady it so it doesn't twist as it is stitched, while keeping your right hand further back, away from the blade.

Starting serging
With the presser foot down, serge a length of chain about 2in (5cm) long, then ease the fabric edge under the foot and begin stitching through the fabric. For a neat beginning on a seam that will be seen, start in the same way, then lift the presser foot and align the length of chain with the edge of the fabric to be stitched; then begin stitching right at the edge, covering the length of chain as you go.

Finishing serging
If you are just finishing off the seam allowance with your serger, or serging to an end that will be covered by another seam, you don't have to worry about finishing off. Just stitch a chain past the end by 2in (5cm) and then snip the threads. If the end will be seen, however, go past the end by one stitch, then lift the presser foot and turn the fabric right over with the outer edge of the seam aligned with the blade; insert the needle at the inner edge of the seam and stitch back along the seam again for a short distance in the other direction.

Using the differential feed
A machine with differential feed (see page 43) is ideal for working with some special fabrics, including stretchy fabrics. With differential feed there are two feed dogs, one in front of the needle and one behind. When at normal setting, both feed dogs move at the same time, just as on a conventional sewing machine.

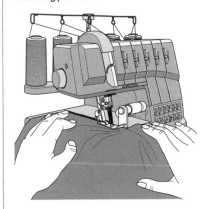

Positioning your hands.

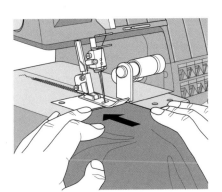

Starting serging for an unseen seam.

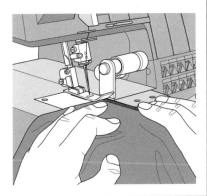

Finishing serging where the end will be seen.

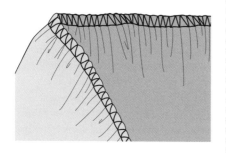

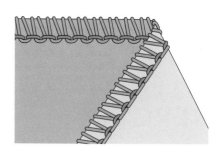

TURNING THE DIFFERENTIAL FEED DIAL TO A HIGHER NUMBER

The front feed dog moves faster than the back so the fabric will tend to bunch up under the foot. This is useful to keep knit or bias-cut fabric from stretching, to ease the bottom layer of fabric to a shorter top layer, or to ease or gather lightweight fabric.

TURNING THE DIFFERENTIAL FEED DIAL TO A LOWER NUMBER

The front feed dog moves slower than the back so the faster back feed dog will pull the fabric through under tension. This is useful to stretch bias-cut or knit fabric as you stitch, to create a decorative waved (lettuce) edge as illustrated below, or to stop lightweight fabrics from puckering or gathering.

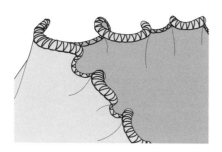

SERGER STITCH GLOSSARY

These are the main types of stitch that you can create on a serger, and what they are most useful for. You may not be able to sew all these types, as this will depend on how many threads your serger can handle and the number of needles and loopers available.

Double chain stitch

This stitch is created with one needle thread and one looper thread, and is used for seams or for decorative stitching, but it is not flexible enough to use on stretchy fabrics. It can be sewn away from the edge of the fabric by disengaging the cutting blade. A five-thread serger can sew double chain stitch and three-thread overlock stitch at the same time.

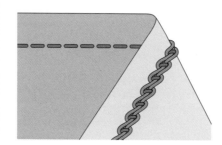

Two-thread overlock

This stitch is created with one needle thread and one looper thread; it is used for seams on lightweight or knit fabrics and for rolled and blind hems. It can be made wider or narrower by altering the position of the needle and is quite economical on thread.

Two-thread overedge

This stitch is created with one needle thread and one looper thread, and is used for overedging, flatlock seams and blind hems. It can be made wider or narrower by altering the position of the needle.

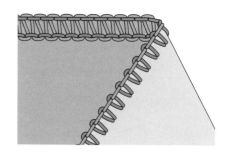

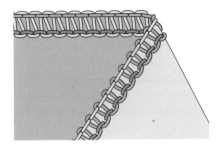

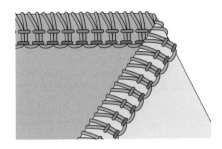

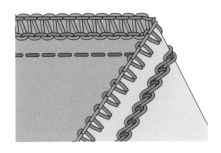

Three-thread overlock

This stitch is created with one needle thread and two looper threads, and is used for finishing edges and for seams. It can be made wider or narrower by altering the position of the needle.

Three-thread flatlock

This stitch is created with one needle thread and two looper threads, and is used for butted or lapped seams. It is a popular choice for decorative stitching when made with an ornamental thread. It can be made wider or narrower by altering the position of the needle.

Three-thread stretch mock safety stitch

This stitch is created with two needle threads and one looper thread, and is particularly useful for seams on extremely stretchy lightweight fabrics.

Four-thread stretch mock safety stitch

This stitch is created with two needle threads and two looper threads, and is ideal for seams on extremely stretchy medium- to heavyweight fabrics.

Four-thread safety stitch

Here two needle threads and two looper threads are used to create a two-thread overedge stitch and a double chain stitch. Since the chain section of the stitch is not very flexible, this stitch is not particularly suitable for very stretchy fabrics.

Five-thread safety stitch

Here two needle threads and three looper threads are used to create a three-thread overlock stitch and a double chain stitch. It can be made wider or narrower by using the left or the right needle.

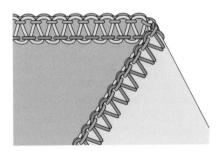

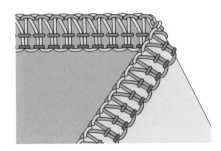

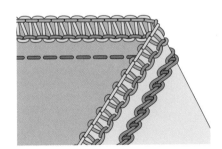

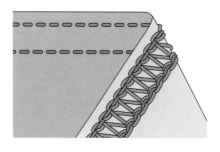

Coverstitch

This stitch is created with two or three needle threads and one looper thread, and the cutting blade disengaged, to make a hem for stretchy fabrics. With two needles it creates parallel rows of topstitching on the right side; with three needles there are three parallel rows of topstitching.

Three-thread rolled hem

This stitch is created with one needle thread and two looper threads, with the tension on the lower looper tightened so that the upper looper thread rolls the edge and covers it. This is an ideal edge finish for scarves and table linens, and for any lightweight fabrics.

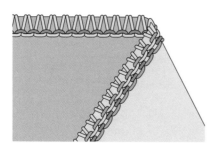

SERGER TROUBLE-SHOOTING

On occasion something may look wrong with your seams, or the serger will appear to be malfunctioning. Usually the problem is very simple and easy to put right. Don't panic – just check through the following section.

> **TIP** Always make sure you turn off the power and unplug the machine before undertaking any maintenance.

CARE AND MAINTENANCE

A serger often uses far more thread over a shorter period than a sewing machine, so dust and lint can very quickly build up inside to cause stitching problems as well as excess wear on the machine. Clean all the lint out of your machine with the lint brush every time you finish a project, paying particular attention to the area under the needle plate and around the looper mechanism.

Some modern sergers do not need oiling, so check the manual first. If the machine does need oil, the manual will show exactly where to put it and the lubrication points may even be marked in the machine itself. Always use the type of oil recommended by the manufacturer. After oiling, make a few lines of stitching on some scrap fabric before working on a project to allow any excess oil to escape.

The cutting blades should last for several years before becoming blunt, but if they are not cutting cleanly, wipe them with a little alcohol on a soft cloth and tighten the screws. If either of the blades is still not cutting properly you will need to replace it. If the blade is not cutting at all, check if you have the upper blade disengaged.

THREADS FOR A SERGER

✂ Always use good-quality serger thread, which is sold in larger spools or cones because a serger uses vast amounts of thread.

✂ A fine, strong thread, such as polyester or nylon, is the best choice. Polycotton or cotton threads will give acceptable results, but they create more lint and may break at higher tensions and speeds.

✂ Use the same brand and type of thread in all the threading runs; do not mix and match threads.

✂ Try to use the same size spools or cones on each spool pin to ensure that each thread feeds evenly at the same rate.

✂ Black thread can sometimes cause static, leading to skipped stitches, so if possible use a dark gray or navy instead. If you must use black, put it in the needles but use gray or navy in the loopers.

SOLVING YOUR SERGER PROBLEMS

PROBLEM	POSSIBLE CAUSE	SOLUTION
Skipped stitches	The needle is too heavy for the fabric being stitched.	Change to a finer needle.
	The upper looper tension is too tight.	Loosen the upper looper tension.
	The needle is damaged or blunt.	Replace the needle.
	The needle tension is too loose.	Tighten the needle tension.
	The needle is not the correct type.	Always use the type of needle recommended for your serger.
	The serger is not threaded correctly.	Rethread the serger, making sure you are going through all the threading guides correctly.
Stitches pulling through to the right side	The needle plate being used is the wrong one.	Change to the correct needle plate.
	The stitch width is set too narrow for the weight of fabric.	Increase the stitch width.
	The thread is not correctly placed into the tension mechanism.	Holding the thread above the tension mechanism, pull it firmly below to slide it into the tension mechanism correctly.
	The needle is damaged or blunt.	Replace the needle.
	The blade is not correctly set.	Check the manual for instructions on resetting the blade.
Loops are forming at the seam edge	The thread is not correctly placed into the tension mechanism.	Holding the thread above the tension mechanism, pull it firmly below to slide it into the tension mechanism correctly.
	The looper tension is too loose.	Tighten the looper tension.
	The thread has slipped out of the thread guides.	Rethread the serger, making sure you are going through all the threading guides correctly.
	The blade is cutting off too much fabric.	Check that the blade is aligned with the edge of the needle plate. Consult the manual if the blade needs realigning.

PROBLEM	POSSIBLE CAUSE	SOLUTION
Serger is jamming	Presser foot pressure is too heavy for the fabric being sewn.	Reduce the presser foot pressure.
	Fabric has been inserted behind the blade.	The blade is in front of the needle, so always insert the fabric from the front so the edge can be trimmed before it reaches the needle.
	Thread is caught under the presser foot.	Clean out around the presser foot. Make sure you continue stitching a chain of around 2in (5cm) after completing a row of stitching.
The threads keep breaking	The serger is not threaded correctly.	Rethread the serger, making sure you are going through all the threading guides correctly and threading the loopers before the needles in the correct order.
	The thread guide hanger is not in the right position.	Make sure the telescopic rod is fully extended and that each thread guide is aligned over its corresponding spool pin.
	The tension on the thread that is breaking is too tight.	Loosen the tension on that thread.
	The thread is caught on the spool or spool pin.	Check the spool is not damaged and that the thread is flowing smoothly.
	The thread is old or not strong enough.	Change the thread. Always use good-quality thread.
	The needle is damaged or blunt.	Replace the needle.

SEWING BASICS

Before beginning to use your sewing machine to make your own projects there are a few basics you need to get to grips with. Take the time to read the information over the next few pages to ensure you get professional results when you sew.

MEASURING AND MARKING

Accurate measuring is very important for most sewing projects. There are several types of marking and measuring tools you can use and although the work you are doing and the fabric used may sometimes be factors, generally the choice is down to personal preference.

Measuring tools

Whichever tool you choose for the job, remember the golden rule: take every measurement at least twice.

Tape measure: for sewing, choose a flexible tape measure showing both imperial and metric to save having to convert dimensions. There are many types: a fiberglass tape is less likely to stretch over time.

Retractable metal tape measure: to measure up windows for drapes or similar tasks, a metal retractable tape is usually longer than a tape measure and will be easier to use. They come in a variety of lengths; look for one with both imperial and metric markings.

Yardstick: traditionally used to measure lengths of fabric, this 36in (1m) wooden ruler is also handy to measure up above your head height because it does not bend as a metal tape might do.

Adjustable ruler: this folds out to quite a length and when locked in place is quite stable, so it is handy for measuring high windows or for sliding under furniture where a tape might buckle or twist.

Seam gauge: this small metal ruler with sliding marker is useful for achieving seams of an even depth, and it is also great for measuring accurate widths of border.

Marking tools

When transferring measurements there are many choices available to you. Your aim is to make an unobtrusive but visible mark on the fabric that will not show on the finished project. Test your choice on both the right and wrong side of the fabric to determine if it is suitable.

Water-soluble marker: marks made with this can be sponged off with water, or will fade away in the first wash, making it suitable for use on washable fabrics only.

Air-soluble marker: marks made with this will gradually fade from exposure to the air, and the time this takes can vary according to the fabric. It may not be suitable for long-term projects because the marks may fade too quickly.

Chalk pencil/tailor's pencil: the chalk is available in several colors and the pencil often has a stiff brush at one end for removing marks when no longer required.

Tailor's chalk: sometimes also called dressmaker's chalk. Available in a range of colors and useful for creating different weights of line. Marks can be brushed away easily when no longer needed.

Chalk wheel: an easy-to-use dispenser that can be refilled with different colors of chalk powder, so you can choose a color that will show up well on your fabric.

Tracing wheel: dressmaker's carbon is placed between the pattern and the fabric, then the tracing wheel is run along the lines of the design to transfer a dotted outline to the fabric. This is one of the quickest ways to transfer continuous lines, but as the marks may be difficult to remove, it is best used for designs that will be hidden by stitching.

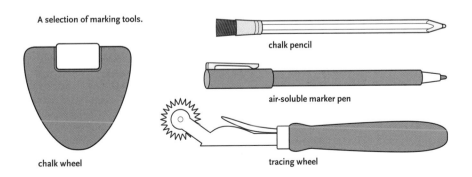

A selection of marking tools.

chalk pencil

air-soluble marker pen

chalk wheel

tracing wheel

✂ Take your time to get the measuring right at the beginning of a project to avoid problems later.

✂ Be particularly careful if you are using a measurement to cut many identical pieces – even a very small discrepancy can cause major problems if it is repeated over and over again.

✂ Copy the important markings from the pattern to the fabric as soon as you finish cutting the piece out. These include any dots marking construction essentials such as darts or pleats, center lines, positional marks for adding pockets or buttons, waistline and hemline if appropriate, and notches if not already cut outward when cutting round the pattern (see page 70).

✂ There is usually no need to mark seam allowances – the needle plate of the sewing machine has engraved lines for the most common seam widths, which can be used as a guide when stitching (see page 27).

PINNING

Pinning holds the pattern to the fabric when cutting, but it is also an effective way to hold layers of fabric together when machine stitching.

Pins and pincushion

Plain steel pins are ideal for most fabrics and for very delicate fabrics an extra-fine version is available. Pins with a large colored head are often easier to spot when you come to remove them – choose glass-headed rather than plastic, which might melt if inadvertently ironed over. Extra-long pins are available for when you need to hold several thick layers together, such as in quiltmaking.

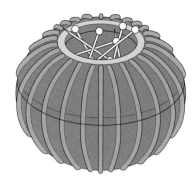

A magnetic pin dispenser.

You can keep your pins in a plastic box – a tin may make them go rusty – but a pincushion saves having to open a box when you need a pin in a hurry. A magnetic pin dispenser is ideal.

Pinning the pattern

Before you start, identify which pieces of the pattern you will need – most commercial patterns have alternative options, so you may not need every piece supplied for the garment you are making.

A1 Cut out the required pattern pieces. If the pattern paper is very creased, press gently with a cool iron. Lay pieces roughly in place on the fabric, following the cutting guide layout.

A2 Most pieces will need to be aligned with the straight grain of the fabric and will be marked with a straight-of-grain line – usually a heavy line with an arrowhead at each end. Measure the

TIP With a printed fabric the printing may not be exactly on the straight of grain. If it is only slightly off, it will be better to use the design as your reference for establishing a straight line for pattern placement. If the printing is very off the straight of grain, reject the fabric.

distance from this line to the nearest selvage at each end and pin the grain line in place first.

A3 For maximum stability, pin all around the edges of the pattern positioning the pins diagonally into the corners. Pin all the pieces to the fabric before beginning to cut any of them out – you may need to adjust positions slightly to fit them all on.

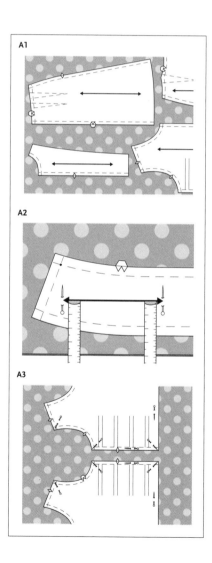

A1

A2

A3

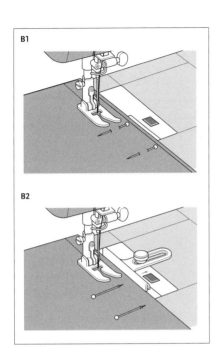

Pinning for machine sewing

Place the pieces of fabric right sides together, aligning the raw edges.

B1 Pin the layers together with the pins at right angles to the edge. Position the heads so the pins can be removed efficiently as you stitch: to the right if you are right-handed, or to the left if you are left-handed.

B2 If you are using a detachable seam guide (see page 51), you will have to place the pins with the points towards the edge. The pin should take just a tiny nip in the fabric at the stitching line and should be on the top surface of the fabric, never next to the needle plate. On small projects or shaped edges, space the pins around 1in–3in (2.5cm–7.5cm) apart. On long, straight seams, they can be set a little further apart.

Pinning for serging

Take great care not to stitch over a pin when serging. A serger has moving blades that will catch on the pin, dulling the blades and even sending fragments of metal into the machine or you.

C1 Pin the layers together with the pins at right angles to the edge, but remove them before they reach the needle.

C2 Alternatively, place the pins parallel to the stitching line, but a short distance away so the pins are nowhere near the blades. This works well for long, straight seams, but is not ideal for detail areas.

> **TIP** Pins can be stitched over if they are at right angles to the seam and the presser foot is hinged, but this is best avoided. If the needle hits a pin, the tip can be damaged, the needle may break or it may even throw the timing of the machine off.

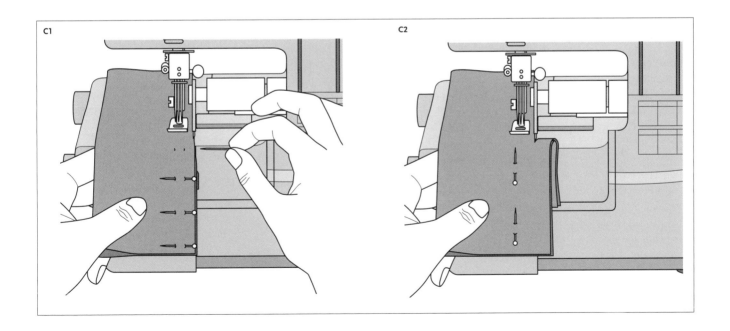

CUTTING FABRIC

The key to cutting fabric accurately is to make sure the scissors are sharp and that the fabric is as flat as possible on the surface while cutting. Cutting lengths of fabric will be much easier and quicker if you lay the fabric as flat as possible first – ideally, flat for the full length you want to cut. Before measuring your lengths, make sure the raw end of the fabric is cut on the straight of grain. With woven fabric, snip into the selvage and pull a crosswise thread until the fabric puckers, then cut along the puckered line. If the fabric has a woven design, you can use this as a guide to cut a straight line across the width. For a knitted fabric, cut along a course (crosswise row) of loops.

> **TIP** Before measuring and cutting, fabric should be pressed smooth and flat to remove any wrinkles or folds.

Pattern repeats

If you are joining pieces of patterned fabric together, match up the motifs in the pattern across the seam. The same motif or design will be repeated again and again down the length and across the width of the fabric, and the distance between these is called the repeat. The pattern repeat along the length may be given on the fabric bolt, or you can measure it yourself: either measure from the tip of one motif to the corresponding tip of the next lengthwise or, if it is a circular motif, use an easily identifiable point in the design. If you are cutting several lengths of fabric to be seamed together (such as for drapes), cut each length to the same number of pattern repeats.

Cutting tools

Good cutting tools are essential for professional results.

Thread/embroidery scissors: a small pair of scissors with sharp points is ideal for snipping thread, for fine detail fabric cutting, and to snip into awkward corners. For thread only, special thread clippers are ideal for both right- and left-handed people.

Fabric scissors or dressmaker's shears: any scissors used for cutting fabric must be very sharp with good long blades. Choose a pair that sits comfortably in your hand. Special dressmaker's shears have one handle at an angle to the blades. This allows the blade to slide along the work surface in a more horizontal position, keeping the fabric flat to the surface for more accurate cutting.

General/paper scissors: a spare pair of ordinary scissors is useful for cutting paper patterns and synthetic wadding, and for other general cutting work.

Pinking shears: these shears have notched blades so they cut a zigzag line. They are useful to trim raw seam edges to help prevent fraying and to create a decorative edge on non-fraying fabric.

Seam ripper: this is an invaluable tool with a sharp prong to push into stitches and a tiny sharp blade to slice through thread. It can be used to unpick seams quickly and to cut the slit for machine-stitched buttonholes.

CUTTING FABRIC USING A PATTERN

✄ Handle paper patterns carefully when pinning to the fabric as, made from thin tissue, they are very delicate and easy to tear.

✄ Lay pattern pieces printed side up unless instructed otherwise on the pattern's cutting guide layout.

✄ When the cutting guide shows a double thickness of fabric, fold the fabric right sides together.

✄ When the cutting guide shows a single thickness of fabric, place the pattern piece printed side up and the fabric right side up – but if right and left sides are being cut separately, remember to turn the pattern piece over to cut the second half.

✄ For most pattern pieces you will be working on a double thickness of fabric to cut two mirror images at once. Pattern pieces that have to be cut through a single layer of fabric should be left to last.

✄ Cut with long, smooth strokes, but do not close the shears right to the tip each time because this will lead to a series of irregular edges in the line.

✄ Make sure scissors used for cutting fabric are really sharp and never use them to cut thread or paper (other than pattern tissue), because this will very quickly blunt the blades.

✄ Always double-check pattern placements before taking that first cut.

✄ Mark notches on the edge of the cutting line by cutting around them as you work. Cut double notches as one unit – there is no need to cut separate triangles. It is safer to cut the notches outward rather than inward as it leaves the full seam allowance intact.

BASTING

Before you machine stitch layers of fabric together, it helps to hold them in place temporarily until they can be permanently secured. There are several methods of basting, including pin basting (see page 69). If you are a beginner, or if you are sewing complex shapes, you may prefer to work with a more secure basting method.

Hand basting

To baste layers of fabric by hand, take the needle in and out of the fabric several times, picking up a small stitch through all the layers each time. Pull the thread through gently until it is taut, but don't pull it so tight that the fabric puckers up. The finished result is like a running stitch, but generally with longer stitches.

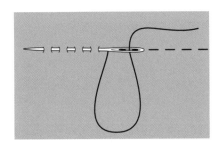

TIP Don't make hand basting stitches too large or they will not hold the layers together securely. Don't make them too small either, or they will be hard to remove.

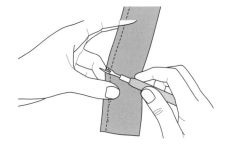

Machine basting

Set the stitch length to the highest possible setting, loosen the upper tension a little and do not backstitch the seam at either end. To make the basting easier to remove after machining, cut through every third or fourth stitch with the seam ripper. This will certainly help if the longest stitch available on your machine is not that long.

Basting with tape

Basting tape (a transparent double-sided tape) is a quick and easy method of positioning zippers and trims before sewing. Don't stitch through it as it could gum up your sewing machine needle. Basting tape is also very useful to hold a seam when you are trying to match pattern repeats exactly across a join. Some brands are water-soluble so they will disappear in the first wash.

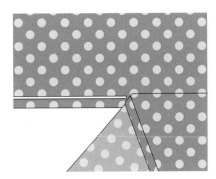

Basting with adhesive spray

Basting spray is commonly used in quiltmaking to hold large areas of fabric together when quilting. The spray washes out easily, but always follow the manufacturer's instructions and work in a well-ventilated area.

Basting with safety pins

Some quiltmakers prefer to use safety pins to hold the layers together. When pin-basting a quilt, work from the center outwards first horizontally, then vertically, then on the diagonal. Safety pin basting may also be advisable if the seam you are pinning is complicated or if the item will be manipulated in a way that would possibly dislodge ordinary pins.

BASTING

✄ Use a contrasting thread for basting so the stitches are easy to see when you come to remove them.

✄ Special basting thread breaks more easily than normal thread, which is useful when you come to remove basting stitches.

✄ As well as temporarily holding layers of fabric together, basting can be used to mark lines on fabric. This is a useful technique if other marking methods would be difficult to remove, or if the marked line must stay in place over a period of time.

✄ You can baste pieces together completely to check the fit, before finally stitching the seams. This is useful if a garment is designed to be very close-fitting, or if you think you may need to make major changes to the original pattern.

HAND SEWING

Even though you may prefer to do all your basic sewing by machine, there will be times when a little hand stitching is required. Indeed, good-quality professional items are almost always finished by hand. So here's a chance to make sure your general hand-stitching techniques are up to scratch.

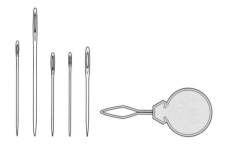

Needles for hand sewing
Illustrated above are, from left to right:
Sharps: these ordinary sewing needles are available in several sizes.
Darner: a long needle used for darning and basting.
Large-eye embroidery: for thicker embroidery yarn.
Small-eye embroidery: for fine embroidery yarn.
Tapestry: this has a large eye for canvas embroidery and is useful for threading thin elastic or ribbon.
Needle threader: for threading even the smallest needle easily.

Running stitch
This is most often used to join flat layers of fabric together, or is sometimes worked in contrasting thread as decoration. To work running stitch, take the needle in and out of the fabric several times, picking up a small stitch through all the layers each time. Pull

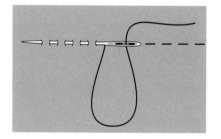

the thread through gently until it is taut, but don't pull it so tight that the fabric puckers up. Continue to make a row of even stitches, with the stitches on the wrong side matching those on the right.

Backstitch
Backstitch creates a row of stitches set end-to-end and looking from the right side like machine stitching, but with the end of each stitch overlapping the next on the wrong side. It is ideal for mending and to hand stitch short seams securely. To work backstitch, bring the needle through the fabric then insert it a short distance behind where it came out and bring it up through the fabric again the same distance ahead. Each subsequent stitch begins at the end of the previous stitch and all the stitches should be the same size.

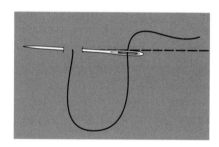

Slipstitch
This stitch is used to join two folded edges together, or to secure a folded edge to a flat piece of fabric. To work slipstitch, bring the needle up through the folded edge of one side, take a tiny stitch through just one or two threads in the opposite layer or fold, then insert the needle back into the fold of the first layer. Slide the needle along inside the fold a

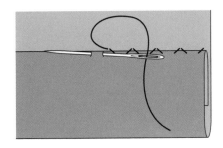

short way, then repeat the sequence – the stitches should be almost invisible on both the right and the wrong side of the fabric layers.

Hemming stitch

Hemming stitch is used to hem by hand. Secure the end of the thread inside the hem by taking a tiny stitch through a single layer of the hem allowance on the wrong side. Bring the needle through to the right side near the top edge of the hem allowance and then take a tiny, inconspicuous stitch through a couple of threads of the main fabric just above. Try not to let this stitch show on the right side of the item. Take the needle diagonally down between the layers of fabric and up through to the right side a little further along the hem. Continue in this way, spacing the stitches around ¼in (6mm) apart.

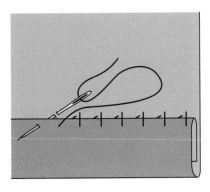

PRESSING

Pressing seams as you work is an essential part of any sewing project and will give it a much crisper, more professional look. Pressing can also be used to mark foldlines, shrink or stretch fabric, ease seam puckers or fuse layers.

Finger pressing

With some fabric you will be able to press simple seams just using your finger. With the seam facing upwards, press the seam allowance down with your finger or thumb so that it lies flat. For a slightly sharper crease, run the edge of your fingernail down the seamline, but be careful not to stretch the fabric.

Pressing with an iron

Heavier fabrics or more complex seams will need pressing with an iron. Set the iron to the correct temperature for the fabric you are using. With the seam facing upwards, press down with the iron until the seam allowance lies flat. The seam can be pressed flat to one side, or open.

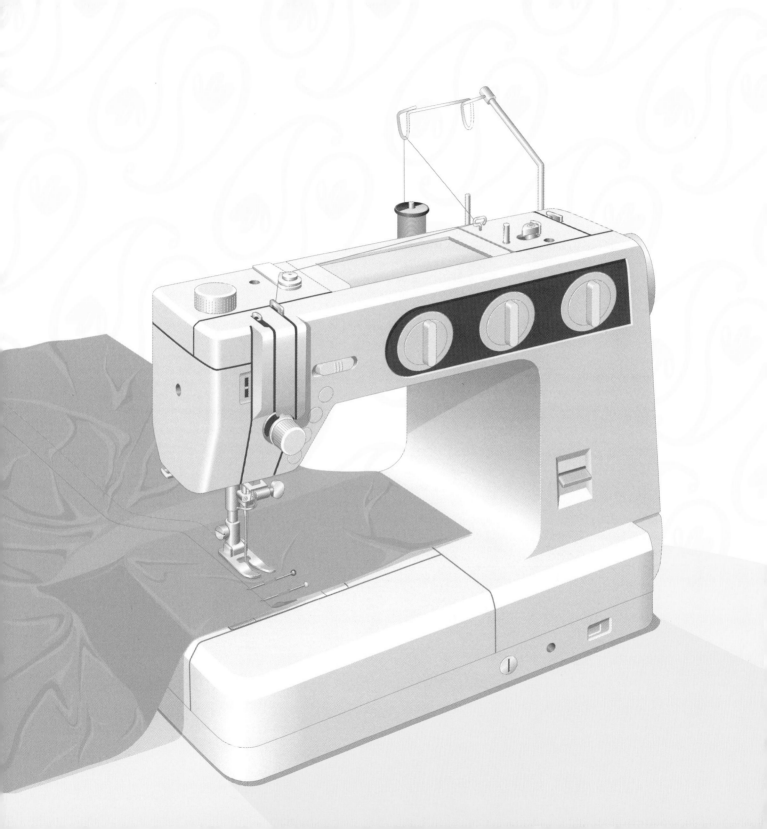

SEWING SEAMS

Sewing two pieces of fabric together to create a stitched seam is a basic construction method for any project in fabric. Although you can stitch fabric together by hand, using a sewing machine will make the task quicker and easier, and the resulting seam will almost certainly be stronger than a hand-stitched one. Although a basic straight seam may be perfect for most projects, there are several different types of seam that are just as easy to stitch with your machine. Some of these are more decorative, or are designed for special circumstances – such as when working with very sheer fabrics.

STRAIGHT SEAMS

A well-sewn seam can often be almost invisible. To achieve this it may be necessary to reduce the seam bulk (grading), and for professional-looking seams that wear well you will need to neaten the seam allowance.

PLAIN SEAM

This is the simplest form of seam, designed to hold two or more layers of fabric securely together.

A1 Pin the pieces of fabric right sides together, aligning the raw edges. There is no need to mark the seamline (see Seam Allowances above right); however, when working with slippery fabrics or stitching more complex seams, it may be safer to baste the pieces together before stitching.

A2 Sew the seam on the machine, using a simple straight stitch with a short run of backstitching at each end of the seam to secure.

A3 Finally, remove any basting threads or remaining pins and press the seam, either with the seam allowances opened out flat – as seen here – or with both pressed to one side.

SEAM ALLOWANCES

✄ The needle plate is etched with several measured lines that you can use to keep the seam allowance an even width. See page 50 for details of this and how to use a fixed guide.

✄ Make sure the raw edge of the fabric is trimmed of unnecessary bumps and is a constant distance from the required stitching line before you begin to stitch.

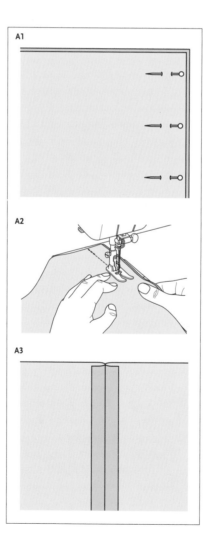

A1

A2

A3

Finishing ends

Backstitching at either end of the machined seam is usually sufficient to secure the stitching and you can simply snip the thread ends off flush with the fabric. However, if you have used a very long machine stitch it may be necessary to secure the thread ends. Cut the thread ends long and thread into a hand-sewing needle. Run the needle through the fabric or along the seam for a short distance, making sure the excess thread does not show on the right side; bring the needle to the surface again and snip off the excess thread.

TIP In most cases the seam allowance will be ⅝ in (15mm), but when working with small pieces of fabric – such as when making patchwork – it may be reduced to ¼in (6mm).

Grading seams

When working with thicker fabrics or with several layers, seams can become quite bulky and they may not lie smooth and flat. To eliminate some of the bulk you can trim the seam allowances down so that each one is a different width – this is known as grading.

Intersecting seams

In some instances you may need to join two seamed sections. Follow these steps to ensure that the seam in each section aligns perfectly across the join.

B1 Press the seams open on each section. To reduce bulk at the intersection, cut the ends of the seam allowances of the original seams into a point on both sections.

B2 With the sections right sides together, match the stitched seams exactly, so they will run straight across the new seam at a right angle. Pin or baste along the new seam so the alignment cannot slip as you sew.

B3 Press the new seam open flat. On the right side of the fabric, the four seams should form a perfect cross with right-angle lines.

TIP As you stitch across the seam allowances at the intersection you will be stitching through four layers. Most machines can handle this easily, but if the fabric is very bulky you may have to turn the hand wheel to ease the needle gently through the layers.

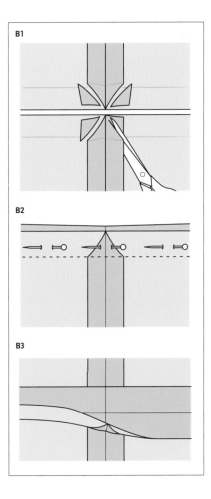

B1

B2

B3

Corners and points

Cutting away excess fabric in the seam allowance before you turn corners and points right side out will eliminate bulk and help you to achieve a neat pointed finish. When turning right side out, ease the fabric into a sharp point using the end of a blunt knitting needle or bodkin, but be careful not to push it right through the stitching.

OBTUSE (WIDE) ANGLE
Clip off the corner within the seam allowance, close to the stitching but being careful not to cut through it.

RIGHT-ANGLE CORNER
Use a pair of small, very sharp scissors to clip into the seam allowance, being careful not to cut through the line of stitching.

ACUTE (SHARP) ANGLE
Use a pair of small, sharp scissors to clip into the tip of the point within the seam allowance, being careful not to cut through the stitching.

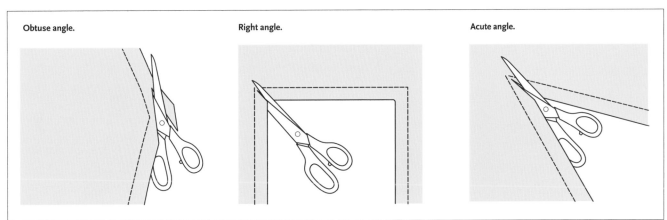

Obtuse angle.

Right angle.

Acute angle.

FINISHING SEAM ALLOWANCE EDGES

Finishing off the raw edges inside an item will give your projects a more professional look, particularly if the item is not lined. Protecting the raw edges of the fabric will also minimize possible fraying and so prolong the finished item's life. The finish you choose will depend on the fabric you are using and the type of project being stitched, so make sure you choose the right finish for your requirements. If you need to grade or clip the seam allowances (see pages 76–77), do this before you finish the edges.

Pinked

Stitch a plain seam, then trim both raw edges with pinking shears. The seam can be pressed open or to one side. For extra security, a line of stitching can be added within the seam allowance on each side next to the pinked edge.
Suitable for: most seams, as long as the fabric is not prone to fraying.
Advantages: quick and easy to do; doesn't add bulk.
Disadvantages: not suitable for fabrics that fray; not as neat as other methods; requires special scissors.

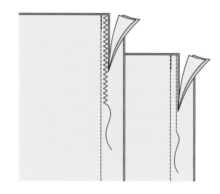

Double-stitched

Stitch a plain seam and press to one side. Make a second line of stitching next to the first within the seam allowance using either a multi-stitch zigzag or straight stitching as shown. Trim the seam allowance close to the second line of stitching.
Suitable for: any seam that will be subject to strain; sheer fabrics and lace.
Advantages: easy to do.
Disadvantages: not suitable for fabrics prone to fraying; seam allowance cannot be pressed open.

Zigzag stitched

Stitch a plain seam and press open. Zigzag stitch along each raw edge. If the seam is to be pressed to one side, you can zigzag both raw edges together.

Suitable for: most seams, but particularly light- to medium-weight fabrics that may fray.
Advantages: effective at preventing fraying; adds little bulk.
Disadvantages: may not look as neat as other methods.

Bias bound

Stitch a plain seam and press the seam allowances together. Enclose the raw edges in a folded strip of bias binding, stitching through the binding close to the inner edge. If the seam must be pressed open, bind both edges separately as shown.
Suitable for: heavyweight fabrics that may fray badly.
Advantages: raw edges will not unravel because they are enclosed and protected.
Disadvantages: time consuming; adds bulk.

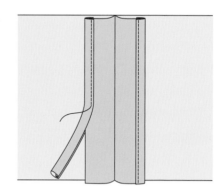

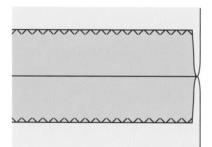

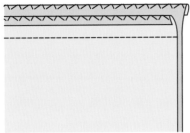

Turned and zigzagged

Stitch a plain seam and press open.
Turn under a very narrow hem along each
raw edge and zigzag close to the fold.
Suitable for: lightweight fabrics or fabrics
that tend to fray.
Advantages: looks neater than a plain
zigzag stitched edge; will prevent fraying.
Disadvantages: takes extra time; adds
some bulk.

Edgestitched

Also known as a turned and stitched
edge or clean-finished edge. Stitch
a plain seam and press open. Turn
under a very narrow hem along each raw
edge and straight stitch near the fold.
Suitable for: light- to medium-weight
fabrics only.
Advantages: makes a clean, neat finish.
Disadvantages: adds some bulk;
requires precision stitching.

Hand oversewn

Stitch a plain seam and press open.
Turn under a very narrow hem along
each raw edge and oversew evenly
by hand along the edge.
Suitable for: heavier fabrics.
Advantages: will prevent fraying
and does not add bulk.
Disadvantages: time consuming;
can look untidy unless hand stitching
is very even.

Hand hemmed

Stitch a plain seam and press open.
Turn under a very narrow double hem
along each raw edge and hemstitch
(see page 73) in place.
Suitable for: very delicate fabrics.
Advantages: makes a very clean,
neat finish.
Disadvantages: adds bulk; very time
consuming to do.

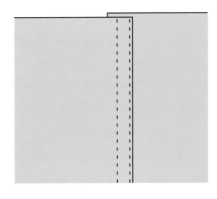

LAPPED SEAM

This type of seam is used to join
pieces with minimum bulk, particularly
for interfacing and interlining, and thick
main fabrics that do not fray, such as
leather.
For interfacing and interlining: lap
the edges over one another with the
seamlines aligned in the center and
stitch together along the seamline.
For main fabrics: lap the edges over one
another with the seamlines aligned in
the center and stitch together along the
seamline. Trim the seam allowance of
the upper piece close to the line of
stitching. Stitch a second parallel line
of stitching to hold the seam allowance
of the lower piece in place as shown.

> **TIP** You can make a form of lapped
> seam in knit fabric by folding the top
> layer under along the seamline, then
> aligning the fold with the seamline of
> the lower layer. Edgestitch along the
> fold, then stitch a second parallel line
> of stitching to hold the lower seam
> allowance in place.

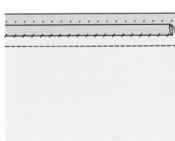

ENCLOSED SEAMS

Enclosed seams do not need finishing along the raw edges because the edges are enclosed during the process of making the seam. Although a little more time consuming, they are the best option for sheer fabrics or seams subject to very heavy wear.

SELF-BOUND SEAM

With the self-bound seam, one edge of the seam allowance is folded over to encase the other edge. It is a useful seam for sheer fabrics where the seam allowance would show through on the right side. The adjustable seam gauge (see page 67) will prove invaluable here.

A1 Stitch a plain seam. Trim one side of the seam allowance to ⅛in (3mm).

A2 Turn over the edge of the other seam allowance by ⅛in (3mm) towards the inside of the seam and press. Turn this pressed edge over again, covering the raw edge of the other seam allowance. Place the folded edge so that it just covers the original seamline.

A3 Stitching through the layers of seam allowance only, stitch close to the folded edge. Press the seam allowance to one side.

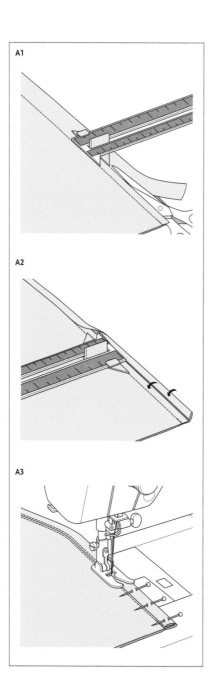

FRENCH SEAM

This is ideal for sheer fabrics, but it cannot be stitched on a curved edge.

B1 With wrong sides together, stitch the seam ⅜in (9mm) from the edge. Trim the seam allowance to a scant ⅛in (3mm) and press open.

B2 Fold the fabric right sides together along the stitching line. Pin and stitch a second seam on the seamline.

B3 Check on the right side that no threads from the raw edges are protruding – clip off carefully. Press flat.

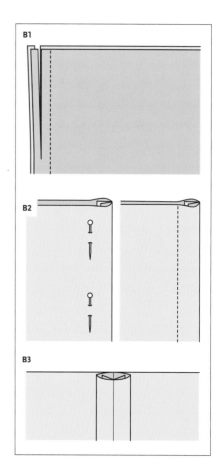

MOCK FRENCH SEAM

This can be stitched on a curved edge.

C1 With right sides facing, stitch a plain seam, and trim to ½in (12mm).

C2 Press the upper seam allowance back flat. Fold the cut edge of the lower seam allowance over towards the seamline by ¼in (6mm); press. Fold the upper seam allowance over in the same way. Turn the upper seam allowance over onto the lower one, so cut edges meet at the stitching line and foldlines align; press.

C3 Stitch the seam allowances together as close to the folded edge as possible.

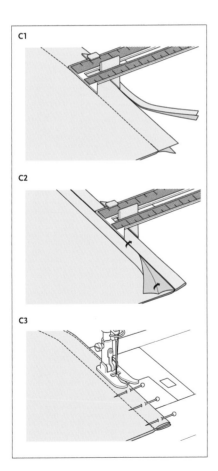

FLAT-FELL SEAM

Designed to give a strong join on heavy-duty fabric subject to wear, this seam is traditionally used for jeans. Work the double line of stitching in contrast thread for decorative effect.

D1 With the fabric wrong sides together, stitch a plain seam ⅝in (15mm) from the edge. Trim the seam allowance on one side only to a scant ⅛in (3mm).

D2 Press the seam flat. Turn under ¼in (6mm) along the edge of the untrimmed seam allowance and fold it over to cover the trimmed edge. Pin or baste in place.

D3 Edgestitch along the fold, parallel to the seamline, through the top seam allowance and the main fabric.

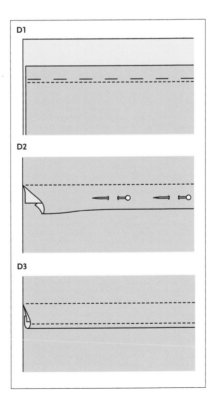

WELT SEAM

The welt seam is used on heavy materials where a strong but tailored finish is required, but where the flat-fell seam would be too bulky. The finished seam is not bulky because one edge is trimmed back.

E1 With the fabric right sides together, stitch a plain seam using the ⅝in (15mm) seam allowance. Finish the seam allowance on one side with a zigzag stitch. Trim the seam allowance on the other side to ¼in (6mm). Press both seam allowances to one side, so the finished edge covers the trimmed edge.

E2 Working from the right side, sew a line of stitching ⅜in (9mm) away and parallel to the original seamline to hold the seam allowances beneath in place.

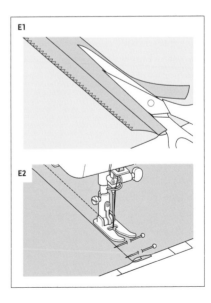

SHAPED SEAMS

Shaped seams are stitched in the same way as a plain seam, but they often need notching or clipping to remove excess fabric so the seam will lie flat.

CURVED SEAMS

Curved seams can either be inward (concave) or outward (convex). Clipping or notching will be required to enable the seam to lie flat.

For a concave curve

To create a concave curve on the right side, stitch the seam and then make little clips or snips in the seam allowance just up to – but not through – the line of stitching. The smaller the curve, the closer together the clips need to be, but keep them evenly spaced. When the item is turned right way out the edges of the clips will overlap so the pressed seam will lie flat.

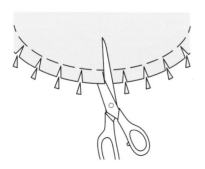

For a convex curve

To create a convex curve on the right side, stitch the seam and then cut wedge-shaped notches from the seam allowance to eliminate excess fullness. The smaller the curve, the closer together the notches need to be – but keep the notches fairly narrow to avoid a jagged look to the seam when the item is turned right way out.

PRINCESS SEAM

This seam is used when an inward (concave) edge must be stitched to an outward (convex) edge: because of the curve the edge of the inward curve will be shorter and the edge of the outward curve will be longer.

A1 Sew a line of staystitching just inside the seamline of the inward curved piece. Make small clips into the seam allowance to the seamline at regular intervals along the inward curve.

A2 With the clipped piece on top, pin right sides together. Match markings, spreading the clips of the inward curved edge as required to fit the outward curved edge. Set the machine to a slightly shorter stitch length than normal and stitch the seam, keeping the lower layer of fabric flat as you work.

A3 Cut small notches at equal intervals along the outward edge. It will be easier to cut these by making small folds in the seam allowance, but do not cut through the stitching, or any other fabric layer.

A4 Press the seam flat, first from one side and then from the other. Press the seam open over a curved shape.

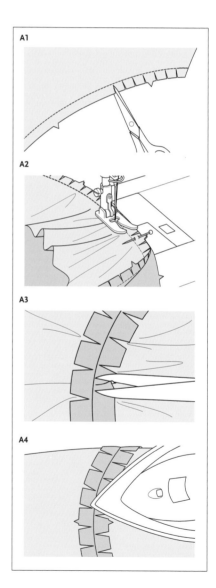

DARTS

Darts are used to add fullness to allow for the curves of the body at bust, waist, hips and shoulders. They are usually stitched first into flat pieces of fabric before these are joined together into a garment.

Marking darts.

single dart

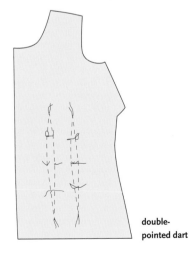

double-pointed dart

SINGLE DART

A single dart will come in from a seamline, usually at the shoulder or side, and the widest point of the dart will be at the seam. Mark the dart line with tailor's tacks. Mark a curved stitching line with basting.

A1 Fold the fabric in half, right sides together, along the dart's center line. Sew from the seamline to the point, and a few stitches beyond. Do not backstitch.

A2 Finish with long ends, tie together and snip short. Press towards the center.

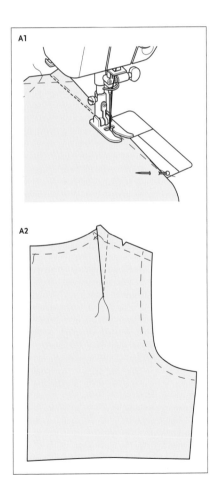

DOUBLE-POINTED DART

Double-pointed darts will generally be positioned away from the seam and normally run vertically. Mark the dart. When stitching a double-pointed dart, work from the middle to the point in each direction.

B1 If the double-pointed dart is very deep at the center, remove a triangle of fabric at the center and trim each end back near to the seam. Be careful not to cut through any stitching.

B2 After cutting, press the dart with the tip of the iron so it will lie smooth and flat to the garment, working on one end first and then the other.

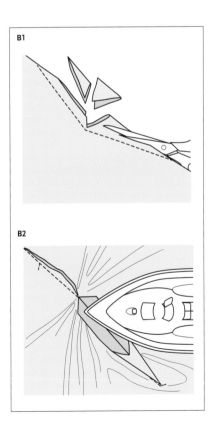

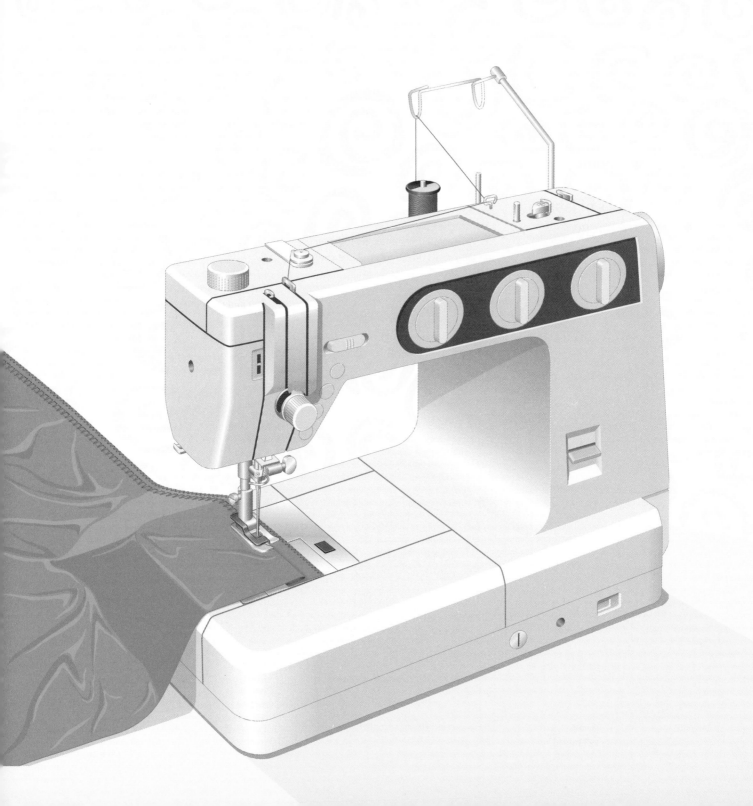

SEWING HEMS

The hem is usually the last thing to be stitched, but it is worth taking time to get it right. An uneven or badly stitched hem will instantly make a project look unprofessional. Fusible webbing can be used to secure a hem on lightweight fabrics or for an emergency repair, but it will often come undone over time. A simple, turned-up, slipstitched hem is probably the one most commonly used; however, you can use simple sewing machine techniques to produce hems that are both neat and quick to stitch. The hems detailed here are suitable for both dressmaking and home décor projects.

BASIC HEMS

A hem can be hand or machine stitched – the choice will depend on both the weight of the fabric to be hemmed and whether the hemming is to be unnoticeable or used as a design feature.

SINGLE HEM

With a single-fold hem, just one layer of fabric is pressed to the wrong side and the raw edge will require neatening. Single hems are ideal for fabrics that do not fray, and also for heavier fabrics where a double-fold hem would be too obvious or bulky.

A1   Measure the hem, then fold and press the bottom of the hem to mark it. Open the fold out flat and set the sewing machine to a zigzag stitch. Sew a line of zigzag stitching through the single layer of the hem allowance, working around 1in (2.5cm) below the foldline.

A2   Trim off the raw edge neatly close to the line of zigzag stitching, being careful not to cut through the stitching thread. (If you have a serger, this will stitch and trim the edge in one step.)

A3   Fold the hem up along the original foldline and pin in place. For an invisible hem, secure the hem in position with hemming stitch (see page 73), or sew a line of straight machine stitching just below the zigzag stitching.

(see page 73)

MARKING A HEMLINE

✄ When measuring a hem on a garment, try to wear similar height shoes to those that will be worn with it.

✄ Ask someone to help by measuring up from the floor and marking the hemline with pins as a first step.

✄ Although pinning is often sufficient to hold a hem until it is stitched, basting it in place will ensure accuracy and a straight line.

✄ Once basted, try the garment on again to check the length before final stitching.

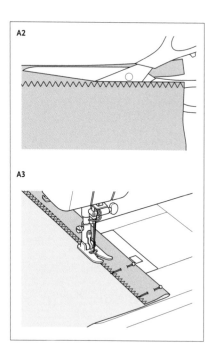

A2

A3

DOUBLE HAND-STITCHED HEM

With a double hem, the edge is folded twice, so the raw edge is enclosed and there is no need to neaten it. A double hem is also a good way to incorporate extra fabric in the hem to allow for the item to be lengthened later.

B1   Measure the hem, then fold and press along the hemline to mark it.

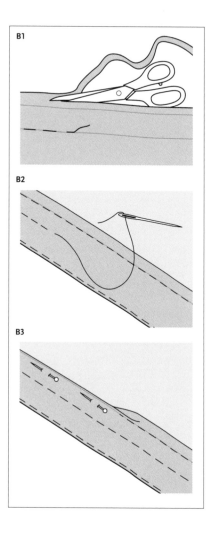

B1

B2

B3

Fold over the raw edge and press again. Baste along the foldlines to mark them and trim the raw edge to ¼in (6mm) from the second fold.

B2 Fold up the hem along the hemline, aligning the seams as far as possible – you may need to ease in places if the garment is very flared. Tack around the hem through the center of the fold.

B3 Turn under the raw edge along the second marked line and pin in place, adjusting any easing so it is even around the whole hem and all seams are aligned. Hem along the fold, using hemming stitch or slipstitch (see pages 72 and 73). Remove the pins as you work and any basting when you have finished.

MACHINE-STITCHED HEM

A machine-stitched hem is generally narrower than a hand-stitched one and the stitching will inevitably show on the right side. If the item is very flared, follow the instructions for a machine-stitched circular hem (see page 88).

C1 Measure, mark and baste two foldlines, one ¼in (6mm) from the raw edge and the other ½in (12mm) in from the first. Turn the first fold under; press.

C2 Turn under the second fold and press. Pin or baste the double layer of fabric in position all round, aligning any seams as you work.

C3 Working on the wrong side, edgestitch close to the inner foldline, removing any pins as you work. Remove any basting and press.

MACHINE-STITCHED BLIND HEM

Using the blind hem presser foot (see page 28), which is available for most modern sewing machines, it is possible to stitch a hem that will be almost invisible on the right side and quicker to work than a double hand-stitched hem.

D1 Mark the hem and zigzag along the raw edge. Fold along the hemline, then fold the fabric back again so the second fold is ¼in (6mm) from the zigzag edge.

D2 Change the machine presser foot to the blind hem attachment. Select a wide zigzag stitch and slide the fabric under the foot, positioning it so that the needle will just pierce the edge of the fold when in the left-hand position. As you stitch, keep the folded edge of the fabric aligned with the guide on the foot.

D3 When you have finished stitching, fold the hem back and press in place. The tip of each zigzag stitch catches the fabric on the right side so the hem is both strong and almost invisible.

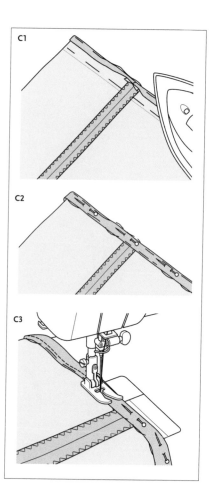

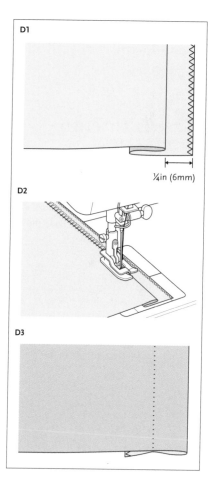

CIRCULAR HEMS

If you plan to machine stitch a circular hem, it is better not to turn up too much hem allowance or there will be excess material to deal with when securing the hemmed edge. These two methods give excellent results, or you can make a bound hem as described on page 90.

MACHINE-STITCHED CIRCULAR HEM

This quick and easy machine method will give a perfectly even narrow hem on a completely circular item. It is a great technique to use if you don't have the special rolled hem foot for your machine.

TIP Circular items should have a narrower hem than normal to help deal neatly with the excess fabric along the longer outer edge when it is turned under towards the center.

A1 Measure and mark the hemline. Trim the raw edge so it is an equal distance from the marked hemline all around, making sure you leave at least ¼in (6mm) width of fabric.
A2 Working on the right side of the fabric, machine stitch a line of straight

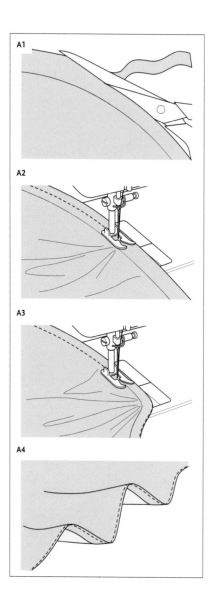

stitching exactly ⅛in (3mm) away from the marked hemline all around the hem, between the hemline and the raw edge.
A3 Turn under the hem to the wrong side along the stitched line and press into place. Working on the right side, sew a second line of machine stitching all around the marked hemline.
A4 Turn under the hem to the wrong side along the second stitched line and press into place. Pull gently on the seam all around to ease any puckers. Working on the right side, topstitch close to the edge all around the hem.

ROLLED HEM

This hem is ideal for circular items or for hemming very fine fabrics such as silk, because it creates a very narrow unobtrusive hem. It requires a special rolled hem presser foot (see page 29), which rolls over a very narrow strip of fabric ahead of the needle ready to be stitched in place. Rolled hem feet come in several sizes to create hems from 1/32in (1mm) to ¼in (6mm) wide. The width of the finished hem is set by the size of the front scroll and the groove on the foot underside. They are designed for fine to medium-weight fabrics – if the fabric is too heavy it won't fit or feed evenly through the foot scroll.
B1 On the raw edge to be hemmed, fold over about ⅛in (3mm) for the first 2½in (6.5cm) and press lightly. To start the hem off neatly, it helps to trim a triangle from the corner 3/16in (4.5mm) wide and ¼in (6mm) long.
B2 With the edge of the fabric folded over, place it under the presser foot. Gently pull the raw edge into the curl of the foot. Begin stitching slowly, ensuring

that the fabric is making a complete loop in the curl. Gently lift and guide the fabric slightly towards the left side of the foot to keep the fabric feeding smoothly and evenly.

B3 Sew slowly to check how the fabric is reacting to being rolled, and establish exactly how to hold the fabric so that it feeds smoothly. Each fabric is different, so test-hem a piece before sewing your project.

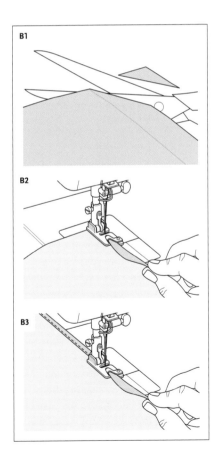

COVERED HEMS

Where there is insufficient fabric to turn a hem, or to avoid bulky hems when working with heavyweight fabrics, the edge can be faced or bound with an additional strip of fabric for a covered hem edge. This necessity can easily be turned into a decorative feature by using a contrasting fabric.

FACED HEM

Facing a hem will give it a little more weight, but it is also a useful solution if there is not enough fabric to make a normal hem or if you want to lengthen an item that has no spare fabric at the hemline. You can also use this technique with bias binding in place of a facing strip.

A1 Mark the hemline along the bottom edge of the item to be hemmed and trim it so it is even. Cut a facing strip 1in (2.5cm) wide and the length of the hem plus 1¼in (3cm) for seam allowances. Fold under ¼in (6mm) along both long raw edges and press in place (if you use purchased bias binding the edges will already be folded under).

A2 Open out the fold along one long edge of the facing. Fold under ⅝in (15mm) at the short ends of the facing.

Match one folded short end to a garment seam and with right sides together, aligning raw edges, pin to the garment. Stitch the seam, removing pins as you go. Overlap the other folded short end over the first, and finish stitching.

A3 Turn the facing over to the inside of the item along the marked hemline and press in place. Pin the facing to the item, making sure that the other raw edge remains folded under all round. Hem along the top folded edge of the facing by hand. Press to finish.

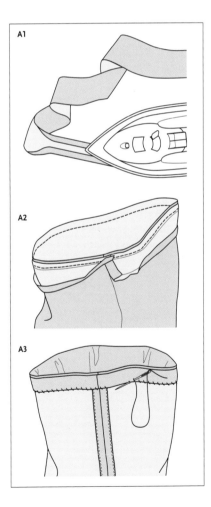

BOUND HEM

The bound hem is similar to the faced hem, but part of the additional strip of material shows on the front side, adding a contrast band of color. Again, you can also work this technique using wide bias binding, particularly if the item is circular.

B1 Prepare the hem and the binding strip as in A1 of the faced hem (see page 89). If you are using purchased bias binding, the edges will already be folded under. Stitch the binding to the hem as described in A2 of the faced hem.

B2 Fold the strip of binding over halfway across its width to enclose the raw edge of the item to be hemmed, but leaving a narrow band of the binding still showing on the right side. Topstitch in place, close to the upper folded edge.

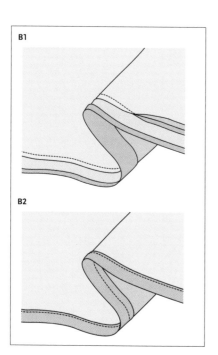

DECORATIVE HEMS

For those situations when a plain hem just won't do, try the following techniques. They are just as simple as making a basic hem, but give a much more decorative effect.

TOPSTITCHED HEM

The topstitching gives a crisp finish to the hem and can be worked in a contrast thread for a decorative effect. You can work one or more lines of topstitching; if you want two lines, it is easier to get them perfectly parallel by using a twin needle (see page 35).

A1 Measure and mark the hem by pressing it and then tack along the foldline. Turn the hem under along the foldline, trim along the raw edge with pinking shears, then turn the raw edge under. Pin the hem in place, matching seams. Baste the hem in place and remove pins.

A2 From the right side, topstitch around the hem to hold all layers in place. Use the guidelines marked on the needle plate of the sewing machine to keep the stitching line the same distance from the folded edge all the way around. Remove any basting and press.

> **TIP** Topstitching thread tends to be thicker than normal because the stitches are supposed to be visible as part of the design.

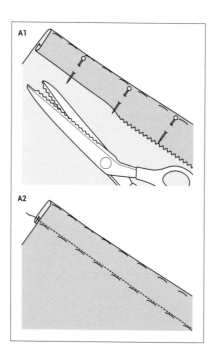

MITERED HEM

A mitered hem is used for the corners on many home furnishing items, such as tablecloths and place mats, but this technique can also be adapted to give a neat finish when a horizontal hem meets a vertical facing, such as on jacket fronts and skirt slits.

B1 At the corner of the item, turn up the hem allowance and press along the hemline in both directions. Open the hem out flat again and turn up the corner into a triangle, aligning the pressed lines. Press across the base of the triangle to make a diagonal crease.

B2 Open the corner triangle flat again

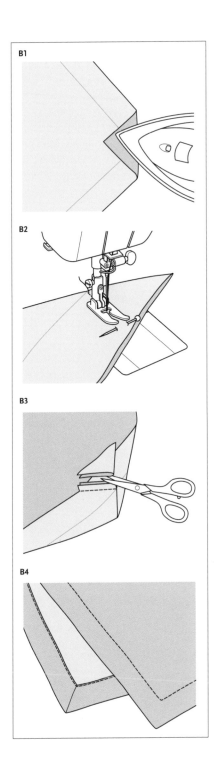

and then fold the item through the corner diagonally with right sides together so the raw edges and the folded hemlines align. Pin in place, then stitch along the diagonal crease made in B1.

B3 Trim off the excess fabric from the corner and press the seam open. Repeat on all corners. Turn the corners right side out, to the wrong side of the fabric. Turn under the raw edges on each side of the hem and pin in place. Stitch the hem.

B4 The finished corners should have neat miters on one side and a plain corner on the other.

SCALLOP EDGE

A scalloped edge creates a beautiful soft finish for both garments and household linens. Some machines have an automatic scallop stitch, but for those that don't it is easy to create with a satin stitch zigzag.

C1 Plan out the scallops so they are an even size along the length of the edge and mark them on the right side of the fabric with an erasable marker. Following the marked line, satin stitch through one layer of fabric, moving the fabric from side to side only to ensure the stitches stay parallel. Try to work at an even speed so the stitches are uniform.

C2 Using a pair of small, very sharp scissors, trim away the excess fabric to the outside of the line of stitching. Cut as close as possible to the stitches, but do not cut through the thread. Press to finish.

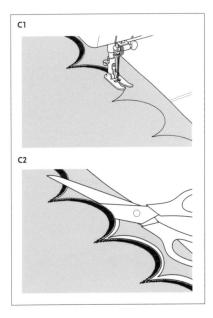

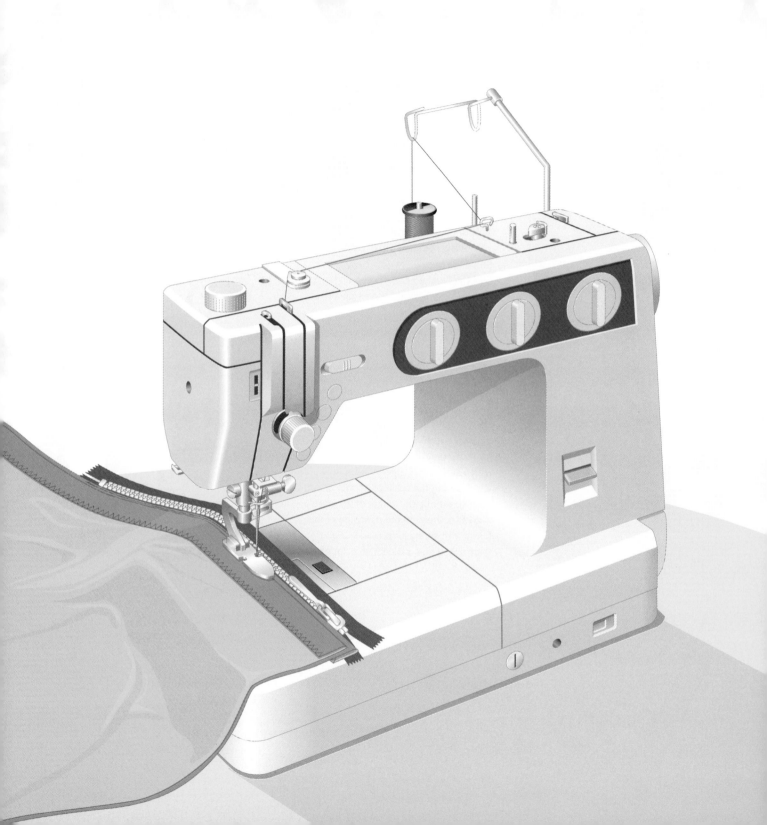

ZIPPERS AND BUTTONHOLES

Whatever you are planning to sew on your machine, the chances are that you will need to include some kind of closure. A closure can be purely functional or decorative too, and there is a wide choice of different options that are easy to add or to make using the machine. Even the most basic machine can stitch a buttonhole or zipper, but this section also includes ties and rouleau loops, which are both simple to make. Changing closures on store-bought items for something a little more unusual and decorative is also a great way to personalize them for a unique and special look.

ZIPPERS

The most common closure used is the zipper. Many people feel daunted by the very thought of inserting a zipper; however, this section contains everything you need to know for perfect results every time.

BUYING ZIPPERS

Zippers can have either plastic, nylon or metal teeth, which are mounted on a colored tape. Closed-end zippers have a bottom stop at one end and are used for skirts, pants, dresses and home décor projects. Separating (open-ended) zippers are used for the front opening of cardigans and jackets. Zippers come in two basic types: conventional and concealed. Conventional zippers have exposed teeth; concealed zippers have coils that roll inward and are hidden by the zipper tape. Zippers come in a range of different lengths, weights and colors.

Conventional zipper.

Separating zipper.

Concealed zipper.

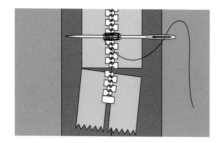

Shortening a zipper

If the length of zipper you want is not available, buy a longer one and shorten it. Alternatively, you can buy continuous zippers, which are cut to length as required.

TO SHORTEN A CLOSED-END ZIPPER

Create a new bottom stop by stitching several times across the teeth using strong thread (as illustrated above) or by stitching the bar of a hook and bar closure securely across. You can either cut off the excess teeth, or conceal them within the seam.

TO SHORTEN A SEPARATING ZIPPER

When measuring the zipper position, place it so the excess is at the top end. When the zipper is in place, cut off the excess and conceal the raw ends within the collar, waistband or facing.

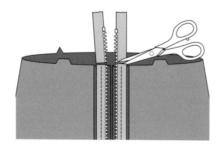

USING THE ZIPPER FOOT

Zippers are usually put in place as early as possible in the construction process because it is much easier to work on flat fabric. You will need to use the zipper foot for installing zippers and the basic zipper applications are described on the following pages. The zipper foot is a narrow solid piece of metal with a notch at each side to accommodate the needle going up and down. The narrow shape slides alongside the zipper teeth and allows you to stitch much closer to them. The needle must be set to come down to the left or right of the foot, and not through the center – this is usually achieved by moving the foot from side to side on an adjustable slide (see page 33), setting it so the needle comes down next to the zipper teeth.

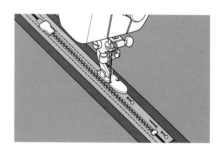

TIP A hook and eye can be used to secure the opening at the top of a zipper to stop it from coming undone if it is under strain. And, if the opening will sometimes be left undone, a thread bar is less obtrusive than the metal eye.

CENTERED ZIPPER

This type of zipper insertion is generally used at the center back or center front of a garment that has a conventional type of zipper.

A1 Measure and mark the zipper position on the seam, using the zipper itself as a guide, and leaving sufficient room at the top for a facing seam. Stitch the seam to the mark indicating the start of the zipper. Zigzag the raw edges of the seam allowance.

A2 Place the closed zipper over the seam on the wrong side and pin in position. Baste along both sides of the zipper tape to hold it firmly in position while you work. Turn the garment to the right side.

A3 Start at the top and stitch down one side of the zipper, across the bottom and up to the top again to secure it in place. Move the zipper slider if necessary to keep the seam straight, and keep the bottom corners nice and square.

A4 Add the facing or the waistband piece to the garment in the normal way and slipstitch the ends to the zipper tape. Make sure that no stitches or facings are likely to catch in the zipper teeth in use. Remove any basting and add any other closures required.

LAPPED ZIPPER

The lapped zipper is set so a piece of fabric on one side of the opening covers and conceals the zipper teeth. Only one line of stitching shows on the right side, making the zipper much less conspicuous. It is ideal as a side zipper in pants or a skirt, but can also be used at center back of a dress or blouse.

B1 Mark the length of the zipper opening on the fabric pieces. Place right sides together and stitch to the bottom mark, backstitching to secure. Zigzag the raw edges of the seam allowance and baste the opening closed.

B2 Lay the fabric flat. Fold the top seam allowance back, but leave the bottom piece lying flat and extending outward. Place the zipper face down on the seam allowance with the teeth over the seam-line and the top and bottom aligned with the position marks. Baste in place along

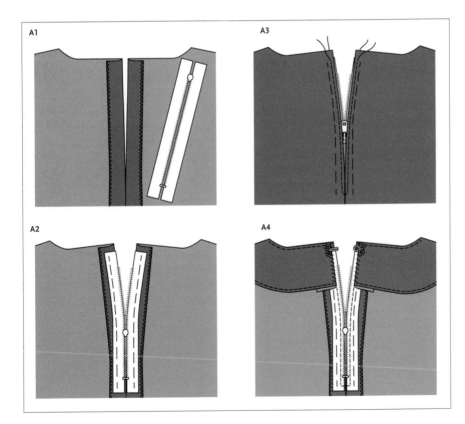

A1   **A3**

A2   **A4**

WORKING WITH ZIPPERS

✂ Match the weight of the zipper to the weight of the fabric you are using.

✂ Buy the zipper at the same time as you purchase the fabric for convenient color matching.

✂ A zipper opening should always be tailored to the length of the zipper, rather than the other way round.

✂ Zippers are measured from the bottom stop to the top of the slider when closed, but because the slider sits on top of the stopper when the zipper is fully open the actual opening size will be slightly smaller.

✂ If the zipper is a little too long, it is safer to conceal the excess at the top end within the waistband or a seam, rather than the bottom stop end.

the extended seam allowance only around ¼in (6mm) from the teeth.

B3 Turn the zipper face up along the line of basting, folding under the extended seam allowance. Stitch very close to the edge of the fold in the lower seam allowance through all thicknesses.

B4 Turn the item to the right side with the seam allowances opened out flat underneath and baste the zipper to the fabric across the end and up the unsewn side. With the needle to the left of the zipper foot, topstitch across the end of the zipper and up along the side. Remove all basting.

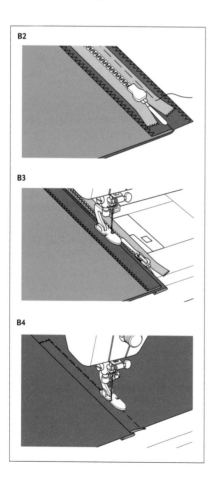

CONCEALED ZIPPER

With a concealed zipper the closed opening looks like a continuous seam, giving a clean finish for special-occasion garments. Some sewing machines have a rolling zipper foot (as seen in C2), for inserting concealed zippers. The method below, however, works perfectly even if a standard zipper foot (see C4) is used.

C1 Mark the zipper position on both pieces of fabric. Open the zipper and place it face down on the right side of one piece of fabric, with the coils running along the position of the seamline and the tape lying on the seam allowance. Pin or baste in place.

C2 Starting at the upper edge, uncurl the coil so that it feeds into the groove in the foot as shown, stitching all the way to the slider. (If using a standard zipper foot, uncurl the coil and position the foot so the needle comes down on the right side, stitching along the tape as close as possible to the coils.) Backstitch to reinforce the stitching.

C3 Position and pin or baste the other half of the zipper on the other piece of fabric as in C1, making sure that the lower edge of the garment is aligned. Uncurl the coil and feed into the other groove on the rolling zipper foot (if using a standard zipper foot, move to the left side of the needle) and stitch in place as for the first side.

C4 Close the zipper and check it is invisible on the right side. Baste the seam allowances together below the zipper. If using the rolling zipper foot, switch to a normal foot, or standard zipper foot as shown here. Pull the zipper tape ends out of the way and finish stitching the seam, overlapping stitches at the bottom of the zipper.

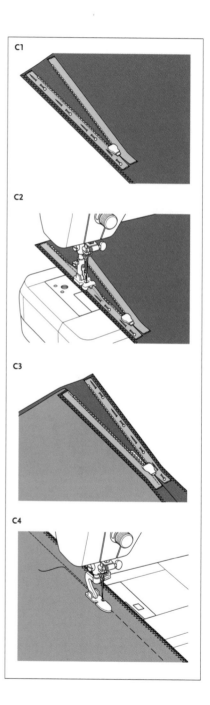

SEPARATING ZIPPER

This type of zipper separates apart when it is unfastened – it's used in places that need to open completely from top to bottom, such as the front of a jacket or a cardigan. For the best result, you should insert the zipper before adding a facing and before hemming the garment.

D1 Baste the edges of the opening closed and press the seam allowances open. Center the closed zipper face down and centered on the seam allowances with the bottom stop and the hemline of the item aligned.

D2 Working from the right side, stitch along each side of the zipper, parallel to the basted seam and at least $\frac{1}{8}$in (3mm) away. Do not backstitch at either end, but pull the ends through to the wrong side and fasten off.

INSET EXPOSED ZIPPER

Sometimes a zipper has to be inserted where there is no available seam – at a neckline, for instance – and in this case you need to create an opening using a facing. With this method the zipper teeth will be exposed, so choose one with colored teeth to match the fabric.

E1 Cut a facing piece 3in (7.5cm) wide and 2in (5cm) longer than the zipper. With right sides together, baste the facing onto the garment piece centrally over the zipper position. Mark the center line and the end of the zipper on the facing.

E2 Stitch $\frac{1}{8}$in (3mm) from the center line down each side and across the bottom at the zipper end mark. Slash down the center line to within $\frac{1}{4}$in (6mm) of the end, then clip diagonally into the corners. Remove the basting.

E3 Turn the facing to the inside and press. Center the zipper under the opening and baste in place very close to the teeth. With the garment right side up, fold the fabric back and stitch back and forth over the tiny triangle at the end.

E4 Fold back one side of the garment and the facing so you can stitch the zipper tape through the seam allowance of the garment and the facing, starting at the bottom of the zipper. Repeat on the other side.

> **TIP** With this technique the zipper is stitched to the seam allowances so no stitching will show on the right side. If you want the stitching to show as a feature, proceed as in steps E1–3 but in E4, stitch the zipper in place from the right side, as explained in Centered Zipper, A3, on page 95.

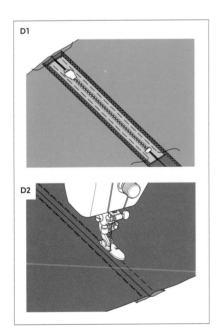

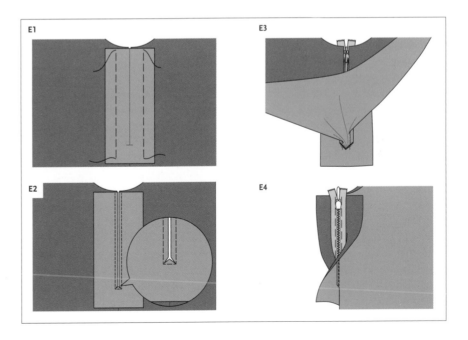

BUTTON-HOLES

Buttonholes are often an area of concern for novice stitchers, but practice will give you confidence. Most modern machines have an automatic buttonhole function. If you plan to sew many buttonholes, a one-step machine with several buttonhole designs is a good investment.

POSITIONING BUTTONHOLES

On a garment, buttons and buttonholes should be positioned so that when fastened the center lines of the two sections will align. Generally, there should be a closure point near the top edge, close to the bottom (but not through the hem), and at stress points, with any others spaced evenly apart. Always mark the buttonhole position on the right side of the fabric.

Horizontal buttonholes should extend ⅛in (3mm) over the center line towards the garment edge, which will allow for the garment to sit naturally slightly away from the button shank, rather than pulling tight against it. Vertical buttonholes should be placed along the center line, with the top end ⅛in (3mm) above the button position. In both cases the button itself is stitched

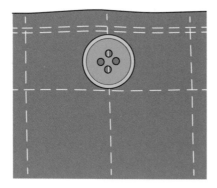

on the center line, but there should be at least ¼in (6mm) of fabric between the edge of the button and the edge of the fabric. Buttonholes are usually placed on the right front for women's garments and the left front for men's items.

Mark the center line and the length of the buttonhole by basting guidelines on the right side of the fabric on the button band, using the button as a sizing guide. If you use a marker instead, make sure the marks will be easy to remove later.

FOUR-STEP MACHINE BUTTONHOLE

Some sewing machines have two settings for a four-step buttonhole, one to stitch the sides and one for the ends. It is called a 'four-step' because you need to change between the two settings as you stitch the first side, the end, the second side and finally the second end.
A1 Use the buttonhole foot on the machine. Run a line of straight stitching on each side of the line of the buttonhole opening to stabilize the edge. Set the machine to zigzag stitch, with a short length and width setting, and stitch a row of zigzag stitching along one long side of the buttonhole.

A2 With the needle down, raise the foot and turn the garment 180-degrees; adjust the stitch width to make a few long stitches across the full buttonhole width to reinforce the end. Work the second side and end in the same way.
A3 Set the stitch width at 0 to make a few stitches to secure the thread end. Pull the thread ends through to the back and trim close. Use a seam ripper to slit the buttonhole open on the center line.

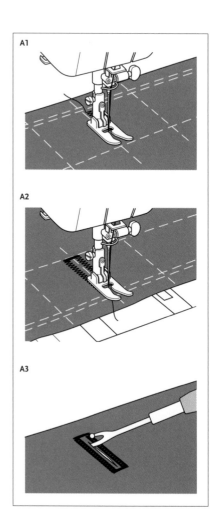

A1

A2

A3

ONE-STEP MACHINE BUTTONHOLE

More expensive machines may have a one-step buttonhole function. A button placed in a holder on the machine sets the size of the buttonhole, which is stitched automatically to fit. Check your machine's manual for any variations in the following instructions before stitching the final buttonholes.

B1 Change the presser foot for the automatic buttonhole foot attachment. Place one of the buttons in the holder and adjust the slider to fit. If the button is very thick, you may need to move the slider back slightly so the machine will stitch a larger buttonhole. Set the machine to buttonhole function as described in your manual. Stitch a test buttonhole on a spare scrap of fabric before proceeding further.

B2 Set the fabric under the needle, positioned above the starting point at the end of the first buttonhole. Note that some machines stitch the left-hand side of the buttonhole first, others the right-hand side, which will affect the needle starting position. Start the machine to sew the automatic one-step buttonhole. At the end of the stitching sequence, cut the thread and move to the next buttonhole.

Buttonhole styles

If your machine has a one-step buttonhole function, it may well offer you a choice of buttonhole styles, suitable for different uses.

Square-end buttonhole: this type of buttonhole is most commonly used on medium- to heavyweight fabrics for vertical buttonholes in particular, but it can also be used for horizontal ones.
Round-end buttonhole: this has a rounded end and a square end, and is placed horizontally with the rounded end set towards the fabric edge. It is used for fine to medium-weight fabrics, particularly on blouses and children's clothes.
Double-round end buttonhole: this type of buttonhole can be placed horizontally or vertically, and is used on very fine and delicate fabrics.
Keyhole buttonhole: this is placed horizontally with the eyelet circle end set towards the fabric edge. It is used for medium- to heavyweight fabrics, and for large, decorative buttons.
Stretch or knit buttonhole: has more openly spaced zigzag stitches at the sides so the buttonhole can adjust with the natural stretchiness of knitted fabrics.

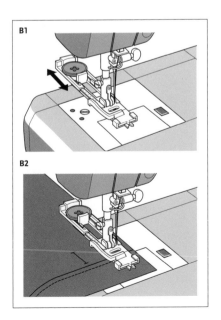

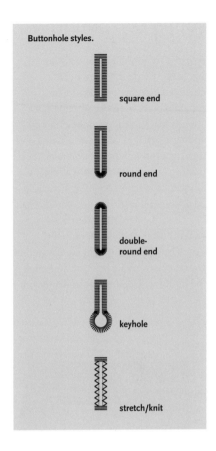

Buttonhole styles.

square end

round end

double-round end

keyhole

stretch/knit

PERFECT RESULTS

✂ It is always a good idea to check the fit of the selected button after stitching the first buttonhole. Then if there is a problem you will only need to unpick and restitch one buttonhole, before making the others to match the new size.

✂ Buttons on cuffs and collars match, but are smaller than those down the garment front, so adjust buttonholes accordingly.

✂ Very fancy buttons with angular designs may snag delicate fabric and knits, so are best avoided on these types of materials.

BOUND BUTTONHOLE

A bound buttonhole has no zigzag stitching around the opening; it is neatened by being bound with a separate piece of fabric. Although this sounds fiddly, it can be done easily by adding a patch of fabric like a facing and turning it through the buttonhole. The binding is normally made in a matching fabric for a discreet opening, but could be in contrast fabric for decorative effect.

C1 Cut a patch of main fabric 1in (2.5cm) wider and longer than the buttonhole. Center it right sides together over the buttonhole position and mark the buttonhole center line and ends on

it. Baste ⅛in (3mm) from the buttonhole center line along each side.

C2 Fold the sides of the patch to the center along the basted lines. Baste again along each side to secure the folds in position. Machine stitch a rectangle the length of the buttonhole and ¼in (6mm) wide, through all layers, centered on the buttonhole marks.

C3 Fold the buttonhole area of the fabric in half vertically and carefully cut along the buttonhole center line to within ⅛in (3mm) of the end, then cut diagonally into each corner, being very careful not to cut through any stitching.

C4 Push the patch through to the wrong side of the fabric. Press it flat and

slipstitch along the folds to hold the lips together. On the wrong side, pull gently on the small triangle at each end to square the opening and stitch across to hold it in place.

C5 To make a slit for the buttonhole, fold the facing to one side. With a small, sharp pair of scissors, slit a matching buttonhole, stopping ¼in (6mm) from the end and then angling the cut into the corners as shown. Align the slit in the facing with the buttonhole, fold back the raw edges, and pin and hand stitch the facing to the buttonhole patch.

C6 The buttonhole is shown from the right side; to finish, just remove the basting holding the edges closed.

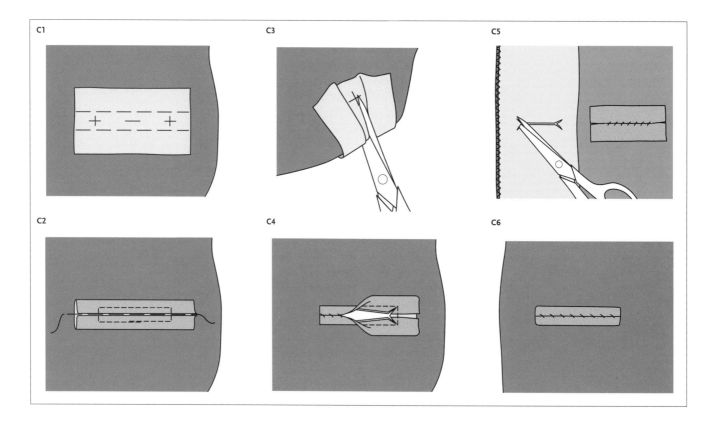

IN-SEAM BUTTONHOLE

This is the simplest type of buttonhole as the opening is just a gap within the length of a seam. This type of opening can also be used in a side seam to take the tie string on a wrap-over top.

D1 Mark the position of the buttonhole and with right sides together, baste the full length of the seam. For each button-hole, cut a small piece of reinforcing fabric 1in (2.5cm) wider and longer than the buttonhole. Center the reinforcing fabric over the buttonhole and baste in place. Stitch the seam, stopping at the end of each buttonhole and starting again at the other side, each time making a few backstitches to secure the end of the stitching.

D2 Trim the reinforcing fabric so it is narrower than the seam allowance and remove the basting. Press the seam open. For strength, sew a few stitches across the end of each buttonhole.

KNIT FABRIC BUTTONHOLE

When creating a buttonhole in knitted or stretchy fabrics, the stretch of the fabric can cause the edges of the buttonhole to ripple or gape. Some machines have a knit fabric buttonhole function that will create an open stitch pattern suitable for these fabrics, but otherwise use the following simple steps.

Use the buttonhole foot on the machine and work with a ballpoint needle. Very close zigzag stitches can cause the edge of a buttonhole in stretch fabric to ripple, because the number of stitching threads in a small area forces the knitted stitches apart. If you are using a machine without a preset knit buttonhole stitch, adjust the zigzag stitch to a longer length on the sides to resolve this problem.

On very stretchy fabric, removable stabilizer is ideal to stop the fabric stretching just while the buttonhole is being stitched. Cut a piece of stabilizer larger than the buttonhole and iron or baste on the wrong side. After the buttonhole has been stitched as normal, the excess stabilizer can be cut or torn away so the drape of the fabric is not affected.

To stabilize the buttonhole edges permanently, you can cord the edges with a length of strong thread and stitch the zigzag stitches over it. Some machines have the facility to loop the thread around the automatic buttonhole foot attachment so it is incorporated automatically as you stitch the buttonhole, but otherwise just lay the thread on the fabric and hold it in place as you stitch. When you've finished sewing the buttonhole, pull both cord ends until the loop is hidden in the end bar tack. With a hand-sewing needle, draw the ends of the cord to the underside and stitch them in to hide them.

> **TIP** Try cording the buttonhole with a length of very thin elastic, which will 'remember' the shape even after buttoning and unbuttoning many times.

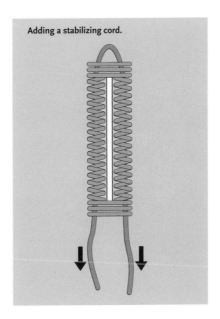

D1

D2

Adding a stabilizing cord.

EYELET BUTTONHOLE

The eyelet buttonhole is completely circular and can be used for military-style buttons, for decoration, or to create belt holes. If your machine has more than one buttonhole design, it probably has an automatic eyelet function too. If not, you may be able to adapt one of the standard embroidery stitches. Always stitch a test eyelet on a scrap piece of fabric before working on the final project.

Use the satin stitch or embroidery foot on the machine. Mark the center of the eyelet position on the right side of the fabric. Stitch around the eyelet using the automatic eyelet function. Alternatively, set the stitch to zigzag with a short length and width, drop or cover the feed dog, and stitch slowly around the eyelet mark working in a circle. Punch out the center of the eyelet with a fabric punch, or use sharp-pointed scissors.

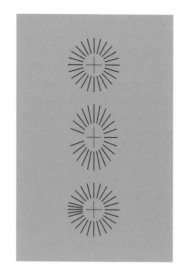

TOP **A perfect eyelet buttonhole.**
CENTER **If the eyelet is elongated with missing stitches at each side, reduce the stitch length.**
BOTTOM **If the stitches overlap at the sides and the eyelet is squashed, increase the stitch length.**

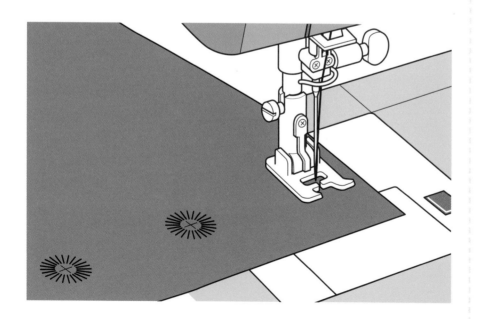

OTHER CLOSURES

There are several other types of closure that you can make using your sewing machine. Ties can be attached to each side of an opening and tied in a bow, but the fabric tube can also be used to create spaghetti straps, belt loops or rouleau loops – an alternative to buttonholes.

TIES

Ties can be made from the same fabric as the project, or in a contrast fabric, or from ribbon. Don't make fabric ties too narrow or they will be hard to turn right side out after stitching. If the ties are long it can be hard to achieve a neat point at the finished end, so it may be better to finish off after the tie has been turned the right way out.

To make rounded ties

A1 Cut the tie on the straight of grain from a length of fabric, making it the length and width required plus 1¼in (3cm) extra on both measurements for seam allowances. Cut a length of spare cord slightly more than twice the length of the tie.

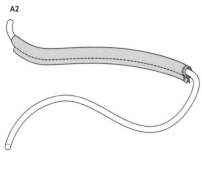

A2

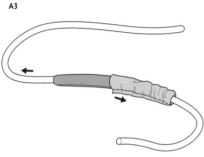

A3

A2 Fold the tie in half lengthwise with right sides together over one end of the cord. Stitch the long seam, being careful not to catch the cord in the stitching. Stitch several times across one end only, to secure the cord in place.

A3 Trim the seam allowances, then turn the tie right side out by pulling slowly and carefully on the enclosed cord. For rounded ties, leave the cord in place and just trim the excess away from the finished end.

To make flat ties

Omit the cord and turn the fabric tube right side out by threading a tapestry needle with strong thread and attaching it to the finished end of the tube. Pass the needle through the tube to turn it gradually inside out.

ROULEAU LOOPS

One or more rouleau loops can be used instead of buttonholes, but note that in garments the edge of the overlapping side must be slightly behind the center line of the garment, because the loops protrude from the edge seam.

B1 To establish the length of fabric tube for a button loop, mark the seamline on a piece of paper, then center the button on the seamline and lay the tubing around it. Make a line parallel with the seamline to set the outer curve of each tubing loop. Make a second line on the other side of the seamline and ¼in (6mm) away to mark the loop ends. Cut the loops to this template.

B2 To make a continuous row of loops you can fold the strip of tubing around within the seam allowance. Use a strip of masking tape to keep the tubing in position as you make further loops along the edge. Note that at this stage the loops point away from the fabric edge. Baste the ends of the loops in place and remove the masking tape.

B3 With right sides together, pin a facing over the row of loops, aligning raw edges. Stitch the facing in place along the seamline. Turn the facing to the wrong side so the loops protrude from the finished edge.

B4 The loops can be spaced right next to one another as shown, or spaced apart like normal button closures. A flat-face rounded button is the best type for this closure.

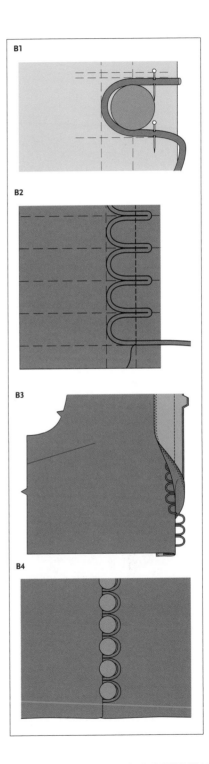

B1

B2

B3

B4

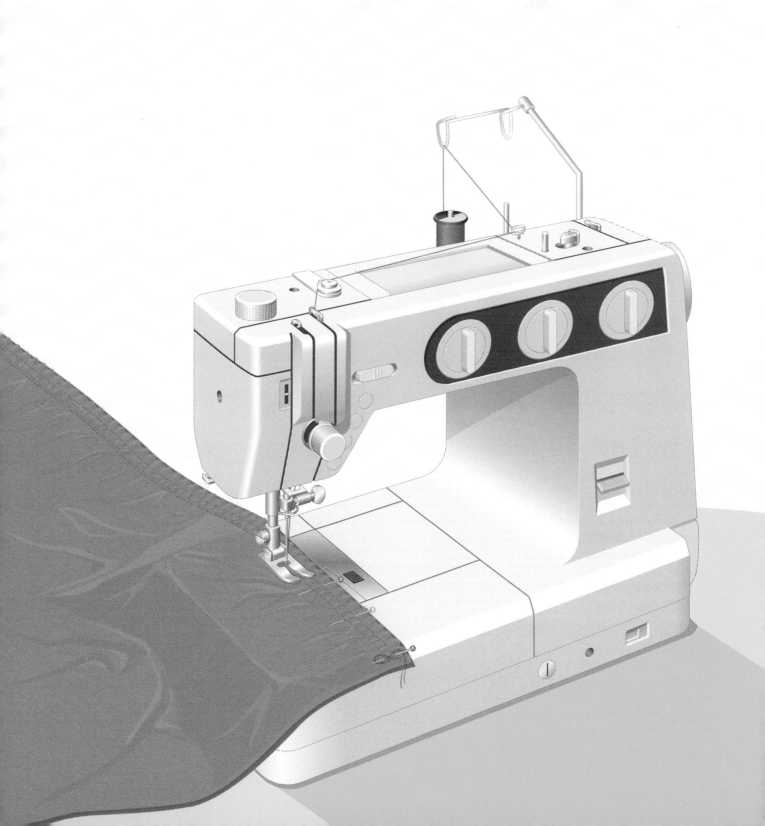

GATHERS, TUCKS AND PLEATS

Gathers, tucks and pleats are sometimes used to control the fullness of fabric, but they can also be decorative. Gathers can be quite soft and unstructured and fabric can be gathered by hand on a short length, but for longer lengths machine gathering is quicker and will be more even. Pleats are folds in fabric held in place at the top, with the length of the pleat pressed in a straight line, while tucks are generally stitched from one end to the other. Pleats and tucks rely on accuracy and crispness, so stitching them by machine is really the best option.

GATHERS

Gathering fabric is a simple technique that can be used in many situations: at the waistband of skirts or pants to reduce fabric width at the waistline; at drape headings to soften the effect; or to make frills to trim garments and household linens.

STRAIGHT STITCH GATHERING

Gathering with machine stitching using a long stitch will give the most even result. Use strong, good-quality thread, but don't worry about color matching because the stitches will not be seen on the final item.

A1 Set the stitch length on the machine at its longest and loosen the upper tension slightly. Stitch a straight line just inside the seamline, then stitch a parallel line around ¼in (6mm) away within the seam allowance.

A2 At one end of the stitching, tie the two top threads together on the right side of the fabric and the two bobbin threads together on the wrong side. This will stop the fabric from sliding off the stitching as you begin to gather.

A3 At the untied end, pull both bobbin threads together to gather up the fabric to the required length, easing the fabric along the threads. Fasten off the bobbin threads to secure the end, then adjust the gathers along the length so they are even.

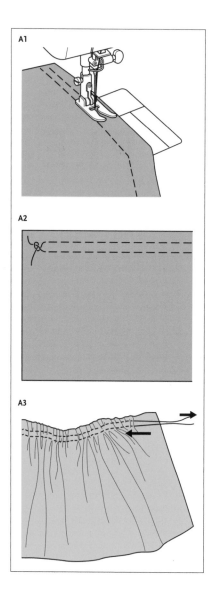

Gathering with a presser foot attachment

Some sewing machines have a simple gathering foot that can be bought as an extra attachment, but creating a gather around every ⅛in (3mm) is often the best this will do. Tightening the upper tension and setting a short stitch length will give the fullest gathers. This foot is a great timesaver when you have lots of frills to make, but the results won't look the same as gathering by pulling the stitching threads as described in Straight Stitch Gathering, and it is also much harder to gather to a specified length.

The optional ruffling foot is a better buy. It can either gather or pleat the fabric, and has an adjustable setting so you can gather on every stitch, every second stitch, every third stitch, etc. The stitch length will also affect the fullness of the gathers – a short stitch will produce more fullness, a long stitch less.

TIP Use strong thread or it may break when you need to pull on it to create the gathers or to adjust them so they are a little tighter.

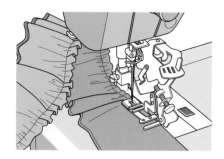

Joining gathered and flat fabric

In most cases the gathered edge must be joined to a flat piece of fabric. If it is a frill to be inserted into a seam, see page 108.

B1 With right sides together, pin the gathered edge to the flat edge, matching any notches, marks or seams. Check the gathers are even along the length and adjust if necessary. Once correctly adjusted, you can secure the gathering threads in a figure of eight around the final pin.

B2 With the machine at normal stitch setting and tension, place the fabric in the machine with the gathered side uppermost. Stitch along the seamline. Unpick and remove any gathering threads showing on the right side after the seam has been stitched.

Gathering over cord

When gathering a very long length – such as around a valance – it is safer to gather over a cord because threads may break under strain.

C1 Cut a length of thin cord slightly longer than the length to be gathered. Set a wide zigzag stitch. On the wrong side, place the cord within the seam allowance and position it under the presser foot so the left swing of the needle falls short of the seamline. Stitch over the cord for the length to be gathered. Hold the cord taut and slide the fabric along it. Even out the gathers.

C2 Pin the gathered edge to the flat edge with right sides together, matching any marks. Set the machine stitch back to normal. Working with the gathered side upwards, sew along the seamline,

being careful not to catch the cord in the stitching. When the seam is completely stitched, gently pull out the cord.

GATHERING WITH ELASTIC

Elastic can be machine stitched directly to the fabric and is ideal if the gathering needs to stretch to allow a garment to be put on.

D1 Cut the elastic so it is the correct length when not stretched, and join the ends if necessary by overlapping them by about ½in (12mm) and stitching together. Pin the elastic to the fabric at evenly spaced points.

D2 Pull the elastic taut against the fabric to place one or more pins in between the first ones. Set the machine

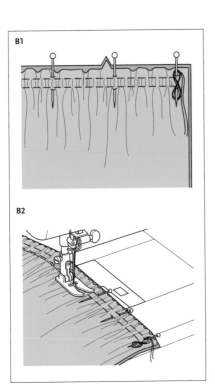

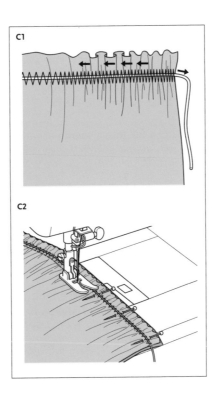

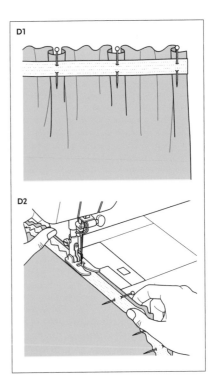

to zigzag with a fairly long stitch length and width. Stitch between the pins with the elastic uppermost, stretching the section you are stitching between your hands as you sew to keep it taut against the fabric.

Machining with shirring elastic

Shirring elastic is a thin, stretchy cord, and it is usually used in parallel rows on the yoke or at the cuffs of garments. Use shirring elastic in place of the bobbin thread and a normal sewing thread for the needle thread. Wind the shirring elastic onto the bobbin by hand, stretching it very slightly as you do so. Using a long stitch, machine a row of stitching; then stitch further parallel rows, stretching the fabric flat each time so the shirring will be even. You can gently pull the elastic threads at the end to increase the fullness of the gathers.

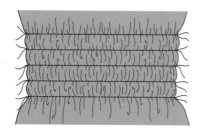

FRILLS

Frills, or ruffles, can soften an edge and add extra interest on plain fabrics.

Making a separate frill

To make a frill with two finished edges that is stitched on afterwards:

E1 Cut a strip of fabric the desired width of the frill or ruffle, plus an extra 1¼in (3cm) for seam allowances. Fold over one long raw edge twice and hem or topstitch to hold in place. Run a double parallel line of gathering stitch (see page 106) along the other long raw edge, within the seam allowance but nearer the raw edge.

E2 Knot together the two gathering threads on the right side at one end of the line of stitching, then repeat for the matching two threads on the wrong side, as shown here. Fold the raw edge over twice and hem or topstitch close to the bottom fold, making sure you don't catch the gathering threads in the stitching.

E3 Holding the unknotted ends of only the bobbin threads in one hand, ease the fabric into gathers with the other hand. When the frill is the right length, adjust the gathers evenly then knot the threads off at the other end so the gathers don't slip.

E4 Pin the gathered fabric to the flat piece it is to be attached to, matching edges. Stitch with straight stitch, between the two lines of gathering stitch, so the gathers stay even.

Inserting a frill into a seam

If you are inserting the frill into a seam, there is no need to hem the top gathered edge as in E2 above. Place the two pieces of fabric right sides together with the frill sandwiched in between right side up and all raw edges aligned.

Making a double frill

For a more solid-looking frill, make it with a double thickness of fabric, with the fold at the lower edge. No hemming is needed, and if the frill is inserted in a seam, both sides of it will be the right side of the fabric for a neater finish.

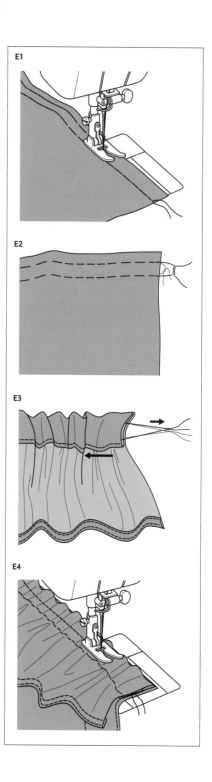

TUCKS

Tucks are generally stitched from one end to the other. They can be spaced equally apart or can be irregular – and the strips between the tucks can also vary in width.

BASIC TUCK

This is rarely wider than 1in (2.5cm).

A1 Using an erasable marking method, draw or baste a series of parallel lines on the right side of the fabric to mark the foldlines of the tucks and the placement lines that the folds will align with.

A2 Fold over the first guideline to meet up with the second line. Press the fold and stitch in place. Repeat, keeping each tuck parallel with the one before.

PIN TUCKS

Pin tucks are very narrow tucks, usually spaced in groups of three or five with a strip of plain fabric between.

B1 Draw or baste a series of parallel lines on the right side of the fabric to mark the position of each tuck. If you use a marker, make sure it can be erased later.

B2 Fold over along the first guideline. Edgestitch along the fold, stitching slowly to keep the stitching perfectly straight. (The edgestitch foot shown is handy to keep the line of stitching very near and parallel to the fold.) Repeat for each tuck.

Using a pin tuck foot

The pin tuck foot, a special attachment for some machines, has grooves underneath that act as a guide to create perfectly even rows of pin tucks. The number of grooves will determine how closely spaced the pin tucks will be. Pin tuck feet must be used with a twin needle.

C1 Choose a pin tuck foot and a matching twin needle so that the needles are spaced at the same width as the grooves in the foot. Fit on the machine and thread up. Increase the top tension to get a pronounced pin tuck.

C2 Mark the line of the first pin tuck with an erasable marker. Stitch the first pin tuck slowly, keeping it straight. Hold the fabric to keep it taut as you stitch.

C3 Slide the first pin tuck into one of the grooves on the underside of the foot to guide the stitching of the second row. Use a different groove to adjust the space between tucks.

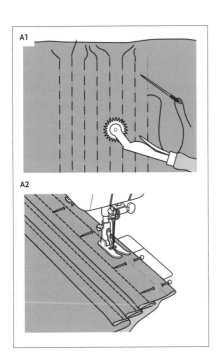

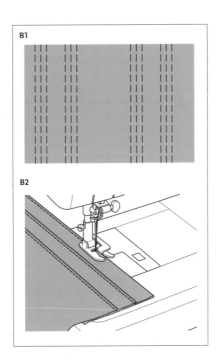

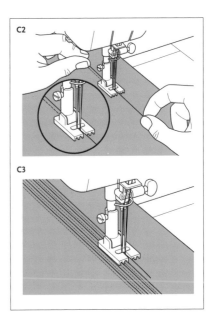

PLEATS

Pleats are folds in fabric that are usually held in place only at the top, with the length of the pleat then pressed in a straight line to the bottom. Soft or unstructured pleats are created in the same way, but are not pressed along their full length, so fall into folds like very even gathers.

KNIFE PLEATS

Knife pleats are a series of single pleats that are made to the same width and all point in the same direction.

A1 Using a marker that can be easily erased, draw a series of parallel lines on the right side of the fabric to mark the foldlines and the placement lines that the folds will line up with.

> **TIP** It may help to use different color markers for drawing the fold and placement lines.

A2 Fold the fabric along the marked foldlines, aligning each fold with the next placement line. Pin and baste each fold from top to bottom. Pin the fold at the top of the pleat in position as shown. Stitch in place across the top just inside the seam allowance.

A3 If required, topstitch down the first few inches of the pleat to hold it in place – this may not be necessary, depending on the design. Press the pleats from top to bottom before removing the basting – for soft folded pleats, press after removing the basting.

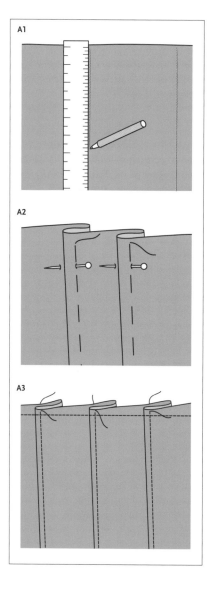

BOX PLEATS

Box pleats are usually wider than knife pleats with each pair pointing towards each other. They create a flatter, more tailored look.

B1 Measure across the width of the fabric and divide it into equal parts, marked with pins. You need three pins for each pair of pleats, so the total number of pins (not spaces) placed across the width should be divisible by three.

B2 Fold the fabric straight down in line with the first pin and press along the length, then bring this fold over to align with the second pin and press the back fold, keeping the pleats perfectly straight.

B3 Fold the fabric straight down in line with the third pin and press along the length, then bring this fold over to align with the second pin and press the back fold. The two front folds should run in a straight line, almost touching.

B4 Repeat B2 and B3, this time folding at the fourth pin and the sixth pin, and bringing the folds to meet at the fifth pin. Continue in this way across the full width of the fabric.

B5 If the pleats need to be held in place more securely at the top, stitch the edges of each front fold together on the wrong side for a short distance before stitching across the top – you are stitching on the back of the pleat so it will not show on the right side.

B6 Stitch across the top of the pleats within the seam allowance at the top edge to hold them in place, keeping the pleats perfectly square. Remove the pins and press the pleats.

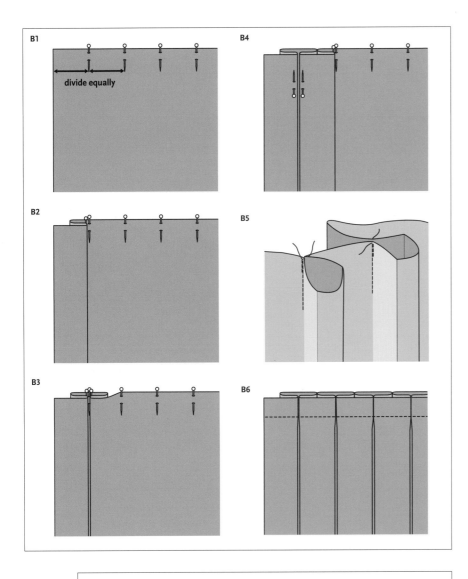

B1

divide equally

B2

B3

B4

B5

B6

TIP You can also edgestitch the front folds of the pleats for a short distance from the top. Work the stitching as close to the fold as possible, using a thread that matches the fabric.

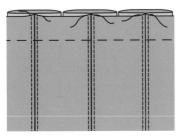

A single box pleat with contrast underlay

This effect can be subtle (below) or more marked, and is perfect for a kick pleat at the back of a skirt. Baste the two front folds together like a seam and press open. Cut a strip of contrast fabric the width of the combined seam allowances; stitch the raw edges together on each side.

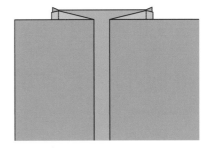

PERFECT PLEATS

✄ Pleating or tucking on striped or checked fabric can create interesting effects and color variations.

✄ Work on one pleat at a time to make sure the line is straight.

✄ When making pleats in fabric that does not hold a sharp crease, press the pleat then edgestitch along the fold in matching thread.

✄ If you are making pleats in a skirt, stitch them after you have inserted the zipper but before you add the waistband.

✄ Pleats for drape headings are created using special heading tape, which is sewn to the top of the drape flat and then pulled up into various heading styles either by pulling on integral cords or by inserting special hooks into marked pockets. The tape stiffens the heading as well as creating the pleats.

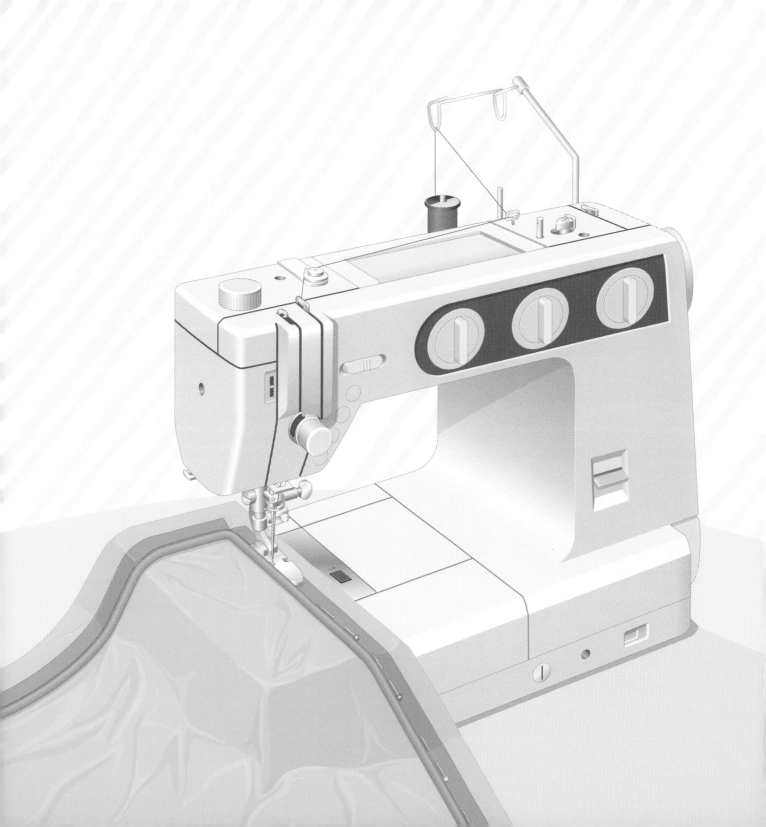

BINDING AND TRIMMING

With many projects the raw edges will need to be finished off in some way, but you may not want to make a simple hem, or this type of finish may not be decorative enough. The sewing machine allows you to add a binding, borders or trims quite quickly and easily, and the basic techniques for these are given in this chapter. Binding is a method of enclosing the edge in a narrow strip of fabric; borders are usually wider and may enclose the edge or can be bound after they are attached; and trims will cover or decorate an edge.

BINDING

Binding is a narrow band of fabric that encloses a raw edge and can be made in a matching or contrasting fabric. Binding strips are cut on the straight of grain or on the bias, depending on where they are to be used.

MAKING A BIAS BINDING

Bias binding is cut on the true bias of the fabric for maximum stretch, so it is ideal for binding both curved sections and straight edges. Making your own bias binding enables you to match the fabric used in your sewing project exactly and gives you a much greater choice than when purchasing ready-made bias binding.

A1 Fold the crosswise grain of the fabric to the lengthwise grain – the easiest way to do this is to make sure the end of the length is straight on the grain then fold it down to line up with the selvage. The diagonal fold is the true bias. Cut the piece of fabric along the foldline to remove a triangle of fabric.

A2 Stitch the triangle to the other edge of the length of fabric to make a parallelogram; press the seam open.

A3 Mark a series of lines parallel with the cut edge, set apart by twice the width you want the binding to be. So if you want 1in (2.5cm) wide binding, space the lines 2in (5cm) apart. Number the bands as 1, 2, 3, etc., along the top edge, using an air-erasable marker. Along the bottom edge, mark the end of band 1 as number 2, then carry on numbering 3, 4, etc., to the end.

A4 With right sides together, bring the edges round and match the numbers, so 2 lines up with 2, 3 with 3, and so on. The first and the last numbers will not match up with anything. Stitch to join the ends with a ½in (12mm) seam allowance, creating a tube of fabric. Cut along the marked line, which will now run around the tube in a continuous spiral from top to bottom.

Using a bias binding maker

When you have cut your bias strip you will want to fold over both raw edges to neaten them. If you are making a standard width of binding, a bias binding maker will make this job quick and easy. It is simple to use – just pull

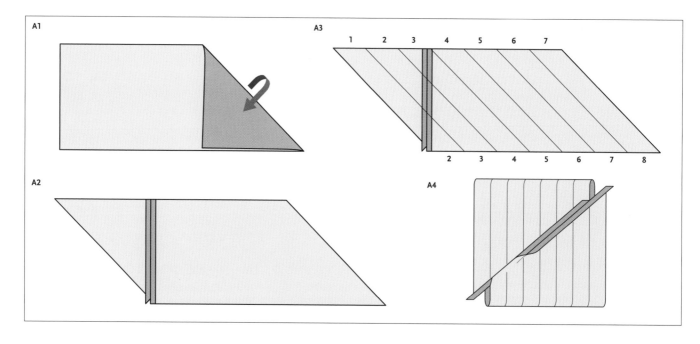

the strip through and it turns the edges under ready to press in place. If you are making very wide bias binding, you will have to turn the edges under by hand and press.

Joining bias strips

For very long edges you will almost certainly need to join two strips of binding together to get the length you need. Join the strips of binding before you fold the side edges over.

B1 Pin the strips right sides together at right angles to each other. Stitch together with a 1in (2.5cm) seam allowance.

B2 Press the seam open. Trim off the protruding points, then fold over the edges if required.

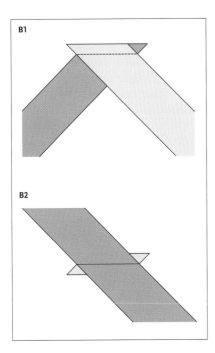

BINDING A STRAIGHT EDGE

When you are binding a straight edge, you can use straight binding or bias binding, but the technique is the same.

C1 Open out the fold along one edge of the binding and place it right sides together on the edge to be bound, with raw edges matching. Pin in place, being careful not to stretch either edge if they are cut on the bias.

C2 Straight stitch along the foldline of the bias binding nearest the edge, removing the pins as you work. Try to keep the stitching line as straight as possible or your binding will not look neat and straight.

C3 Fold the binding around the raw edge to the wrong side. If you don't want the binding to show on the right side, fold on the stitching line made in C2. If you want a narrow border, fold on the center line of the binding as shown.

C4 Stitch close to the folded edge on the wrong side, removing the pins as you work.

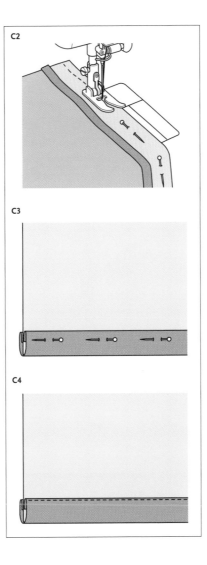

BINDING A CURVE

When you are binding a curve you will need to use bias binding because the extra stretch allows more leeway for manipulation around the curve. Stretch the bias binding slightly along one edge as you attach it around an outward (convex) curve. Ease the edge slightly to fit an inward (concave) curve.

BINDING AN INWARD CORNER

When binding an inward corner, the easiest way to get a neat turn in the bias binding is to open out the edge into a straight line when stitching it on. To bind an outward corner, see the steps for mitered continuous binding opposite.

D1 Reinforce the inward corner on the item with a line of staystitching and clip the corner to the stitching.

D2 Fold the binding in half over the raw edge of the first section of fabric. Stitch to the corner, stopping with the needle down in the fabric at the point of the corner. Raise the presser foot and swing the other half of the edge to the left, opening the clipped corner right out so that the two sections of the edge now run in a straight line. This will cause a small gather to form at the point of the clip.

D3 Enclose the remaining length of raw edge with the binding, lower the presser foot again, and continue stitching to the end, being careful not to pull too much as you stitch past the end of the clip. Remove the item from the machine.

D4 As the fabric is released from the presser foot, the inward corner of the item will come back into position, with the excess binding at the corner folding into a neat miter on both sides. You can slipstitch the miter in place or leave it as a fold.

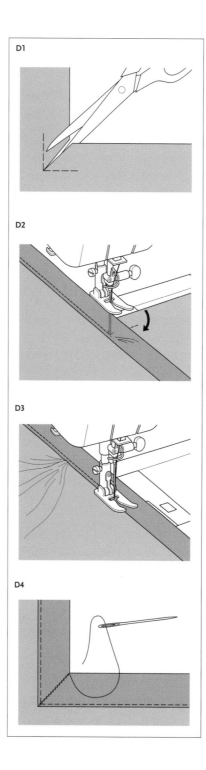

SINGLE BINDING

If you want to bind right around a square or rectangular item, straight single binding is ideal. It uses less fabric than double binding (see opposite), but will not protect the edges quite as well on an item that will be heavily used.

E1 Cut a strip of binding the length of each side and twice the width you want the binding to be, plus an extra ½in (12mm) for seam allowances. Along one long edge of each strip, press a ¼in (6mm) width of fabric to the wrong side. At each corner of the item, measure in ¼in (6mm) from both edges and make a small mark. Place a binding strip down one edge, with right sides together and raw edges aligned – the folded edge of the binding should be towards the center. Stitch the binding in place between the corner marks only.

E2 Fold the attached strip of binding up out of the way and pin a new strip along the next edge as before. Stitch between the marked corner points again, being careful not to catch the edge of the first strip as you begin sewing. Repeat for the remaining two strips on the other two sides.

E3 Fold the binding over to the back of the item along one edge, concealing the raw edges. Pin in place along the length of the side.

E4 At the end of each strip, fold in the raw edges and square the corners. Pin in place. Slipstitch the binding to the reverse of the item along the foldline made in E1 and at each corner.

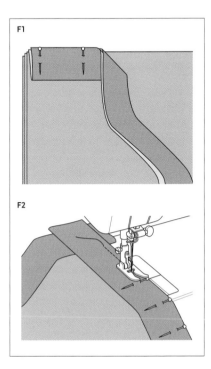

DOUBLE BINDING

Double binding – also sometimes known as French-fold binding – is stronger than single binding, so it is more suitable for items that will be heavily used and laundered frequently.

F1 Cut a strip of binding the length of each side and four times the width you want the binding to be, plus an extra ½in (12mm) for seam allowances. Fold the strips in half lengthwise and press. At each corner of the item, measure in ¼in (6mm) from both edges and make a small mark.

F2 Starting with the two raw edges of the binding aligned with the raw edge of the item and the fold towards the center, stitch the first strip in place between the corner marks only. Follow E2–E4 of single binding.

MITERED CONTINUOUS BINDING

Rather than using separate strips, you can bind the edges of a square or rectangular item with a continuous strip of binding and create a miter at each corner.

G1 Make a length of binding four times the finished width you want the binding to be, and long enough to go all around the item. Press the two long edges over to the wrong side to meet at the center. Open out the fold along one edge.

G2 At each corner of the item, measure in ¼in (6mm) from both edges and make a small mark. Place the binding strip along one edge, with right sides together and raw edges aligned – the folded edge of the binding should be towards the center. Starting the width

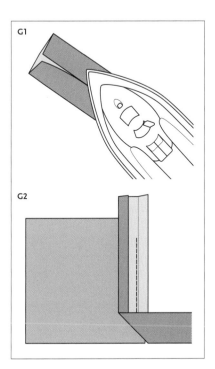

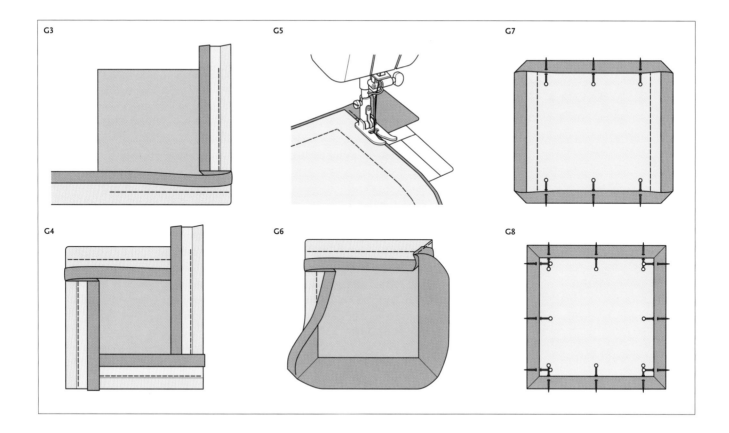

G3

G5

G7

G4

G6

G8

of the binding strip from the edge, stitch to the first corner mark, then backstitch to secure. Remove the item from the machine. Fold the binding to one side on a diagonal line and finger press.

G3 Fold the binding strip across to align it with the next edge to be worked, holding the diagonal fold in place with your finger. Begin stitching again along the second edge of the item, starting at the folded edge of the binding. Repeat for the third and fourth sides.

G4 When you arrive back at your starting position again, slide the last end of the binding underneath the loose end of the first strip to conceal it. Complete the stitching on the first side to the edge.

G5 Turn the item over and stitch across the first and last binding strip very close to the edge. Trim off the excess pieces of binding fabric as near as possible to this line of stitching.

G6 Turn the item over once again and fold the binding over to the wrong side to enclose the raw edges along each side, creating a neat miter at each corner.

G7 Turn back to the wrong side again, and turn up the top and bottom strips of binding so the folded edges line up with the seamline. Pin in place along the top and bottom strips.

G8 Fold over the other two sides in the same way and tuck the excess fabric

at each corner into a neat miter. Pin in place. Neatly slipstitch along all four sides and along the mitered corners.

TIP When you are stitching on binding, be very careful not to stretch it as you sew, particularly if you are using purchased bias binding.

PIPING

Piping is a strip of flat, folded fabric inserted into a seam for decoration. Piping that has a cord added inside the fold is known as cording.

SIMPLE PIPING

Simple piping lies flat and has a soft, rounded look in the seam.

A1 Make a strip of bias binding twice the width you want the piping to be, plus 1¼in (3cm) for the seam allowances. Fold the strip in half, wrong sides together and with raw edges aligned.

A2 On the seam that is to be piped, place the fabric pieces right sides together with the piping sandwiched in between and all raw edges aligned. Pin or baste together. Stitch along the seamline.

CORDING

Cording gives a sculptured look.

B1 Make a strip of bias binding three times the width of the cord, plus 1¼in (3cm) for the seam allowances.

B2 Fold the strip in half, wrong sides together; insert the cord into the fold and align the raw edges. Stitch along the strip as close to the cord as possible, but without catching it.

B3 Place the fabric right sides together with the cording sandwiched in between and all raw edges aligned. Stitch along the seamline, keeping close to the cord.

Joining cording

To create a neat join in cording, pull the end out of the fabric casing at each end and trim off the cord ends only so they will exactly meet at the join. Turn under the end of one length of the piping and slide it over the other.

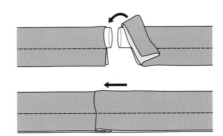

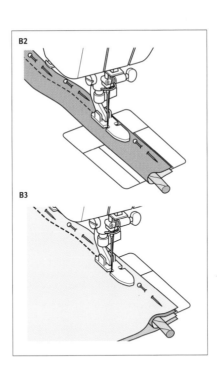

Piping an outward corner

C1 Pin the piping to the fabric's edge. At the corner, clip the seam allowance of the piping up to, but not through, the stitching. Continue to pin in place.

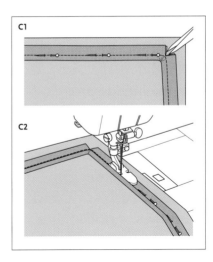

C2 Stitch to the corner. Leaving the needle in the fabric, lift the presser foot up and turn. Drop the foot and continue.

Piping an inward corner

Reinforce the corner with a line of stay-stitching and clip. Sew on the piping to the corner point. With the needle down, raise the foot, spread the fabric open to straighten the edge to align with the piping. Drop the foot and continue stitching in a straight line.

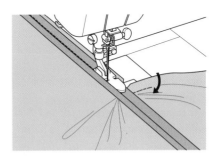

NOTE The piping is shown in the illustrations above being applied to the right side of one layer of fabric only for clarity; in reality, it would be stitched between two fabric layers as in B3.

TRIMMING

The addition of a trim to a homemade project or to a store-bought item is a wonderful way to personalize items. There are many different trims available, such as rickrack, braid, lace or ribbon, in a variety of colors and widths. Trims can be added to an edge or inserted in a seam.

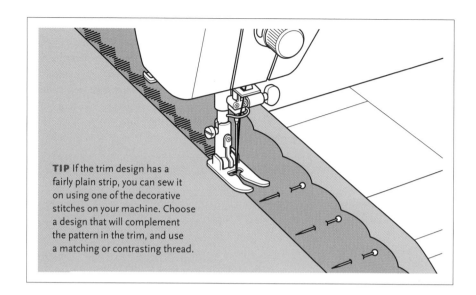

TIP If the trim design has a fairly plain strip, you can sew it on using one of the decorative stitches on your machine. Choose a design that will complement the pattern in the trim, and use a matching or contrasting thread.

ATTACHING EDGE TRIMS

Edge trims, such as braid, are used to accent different parts of a design and are applied to finished edges. Some trims are designed to overlap the edge slightly, some to run in line with it, while others can be inset as shown here. Very decorative trims may need to be slipstitched in place, but those with straight lines can be machine stitched.

A1 Carefully pin the trim to the finished edge or along the placement line. Topstitch along both edges, stopping at the corner.

A2 Fold the trim back on itself and press. Fold the trim diagonally so it runs at right angles and press. Fold up again and stitch diagonally along the crease.

A3 Fold the trim back down so it runs along the edge or placement line and continue topstitching along its edges.

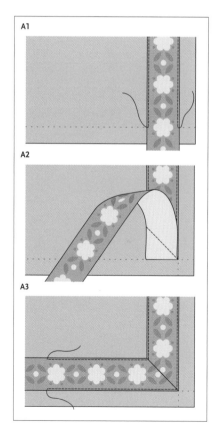

A1

A2

A3

ATTACHING FRINGE TRIMS

Fringed trims have a tape header at the top, which can be used to attach them. Normally, the fringe is applied to the item by stitching through the header, but it can also be inserted in a seam (see Attaching In-seam Trims, opposite). Pin the fringe in place, then machine or hand stitch with matching thread. If the fringe has a wide heading, stitch along both the top and bottom edges. If the tape header is fairly plain, you can stitch it on with one of the decorative machine stitches.

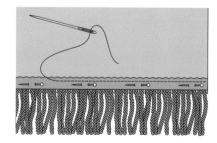

ATTACHING IN-SEAM TRIMS

When inserting a trim in a seam, it must be placed between the two layers of fabric before they are stitched.

B1 Lay the trim – in this case a double frill – on the front piece of fabric, right sides together. Note that the frill is pointing towards the center, so when the item is turned right side out again it will be on the outside.

B2 Lay the back piece of fabric right side down on top and align the raw edges. Stitch in place, turn the item right side out and press.

INSERTING LACE

Lace inserts are popular on both garments and household items, and they are easy to add. These instructions can also be used to insert wide flat braid.

C1 With both fabric and lace right side up, pin the lace in place. Stitch along each side of the lace, quite close to the edge, either by hand stitching or by machine stitching.

C2 Turn the item over and trim away the strip of fabric under the lace to within ⅛in (3mm) of the seam. Press the raw edges away from the lace to finish.

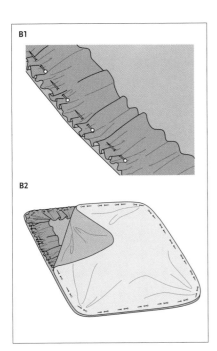

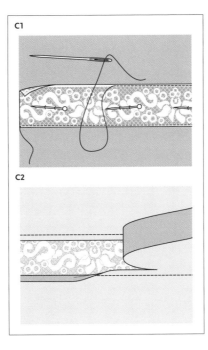

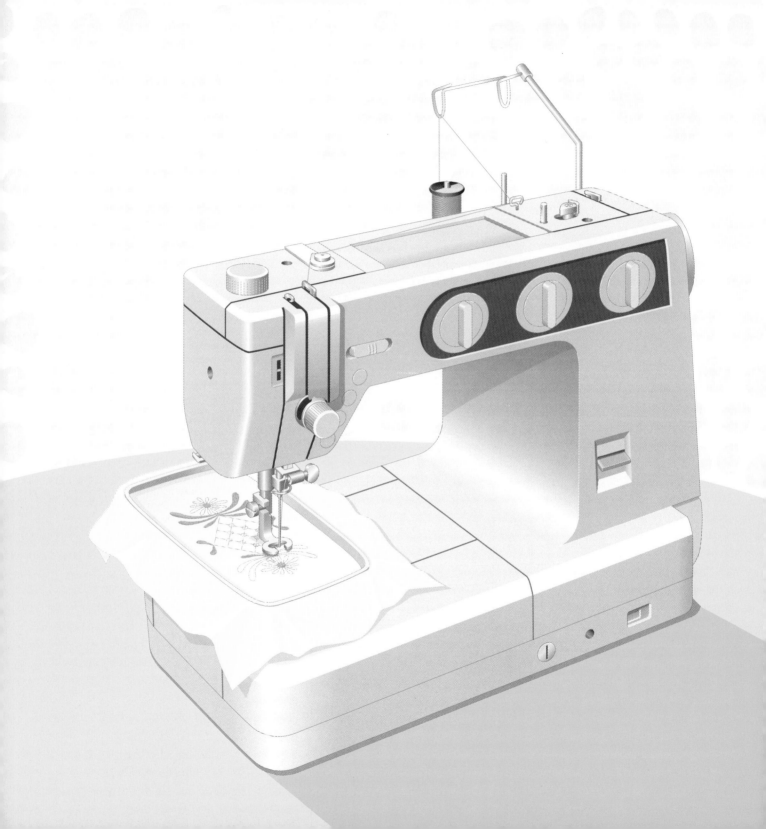

DECORATIVE TECHNIQUES

Patchwork and quilting have long been popular, but a sewing machine makes the repetitive tasks associated with them quicker to accomplish. Many traditional techniques have been adapted for machine sewing, and you can use them to make beautiful quilts, throws and cushions from fabric odds and ends. Your machine is also ideal for adding decorative touches to ready-made items. Clothing and household linens can be made stunning with appliqué or machine embroidery, enabling you to create something that is unique.

EMBROIDERY

Even the simplest sewing machine usually has a few decorative stitches, so to get started with machine embroidery there is no need to invest in one with specialist embroidery functions.

MACHINE EMBROIDERY IN ROWS

Many of the basic decorative stitches on a machine are designed to be sewn in even rows and for this there is no need to put the fabric into an embroidery hoop. Use the zigzag foot or an embroidery foot as these both have a slightly wider aperture than the standard presser foot and so allow the needle more freedom of movement.

A1 If you are stitching a border, mark a central guideline in a suitable marker to keep lines straight. If the rows of stitching will be repeated no more than ½in (12mm) apart, you can use the presser foot to gauge the position of other rows. If not, mark further rows.

A2 Select the stitch pattern you want to use – it is wise to try it out on a piece of scrap fabric first to decide on a suitable stitch length and width for the effect you want to achieve. When you are happy, stitch the first line along the marked guideline. Guide the fabric, keeping it reasonably taut, but don't pull on it because this will distort the pattern.

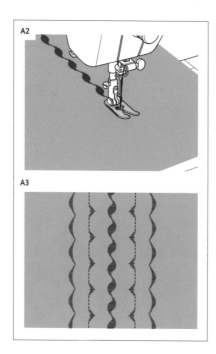

A3 Choose the pattern for the next line of stitching and sew this down one side of the center row. Turn the fabric around to stitch down the other side in the opposite direction – this will make sure the points of the stitch are facing in opposite directions to keep the pattern symmetrical. Add further rows of stitches in the same way.

TIP Use a twin needle (see page 35) to embroider perfectly parallel rows of the same stitch, and save time in the marking and stitching of large repeat designs. The needles work in unison for double lines of stitching. To create a symmetrical design on either side of the center line, you will still have to stitch down one side and then turn the fabric around to stitch down the other.

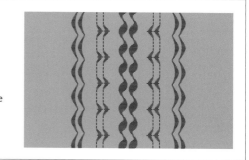

Thread tension

Correct thread tension is very important for machine embroidery – the tension on the top should generally be looser than on the bottom so that the bobbin thread pulls the needle thread down to the underside of the material. However, do not have the top tension so loose that you get loops of thread on the wrong side.

Right side: correct tension.

Reverse side: correct tension.

Reverse side: tension too tight, hardly any bobbin thread showing.

Reverse side: tension too loose, too much bobbin thread showing.

MACHINE EMBROIDERED MOTIFS

If you want to embroider small motifs or monograms, in many ways the technique is similar to working lines, but large single motifs will need some special handling.

B1 To keep the fabric taut when working a large motif, place it in an embroidery hoop – machines with an extensive embroidery function will probably come with their own hoop. Separate the two hoop rings and loosen the adjustment screw slightly. Lay the larger ring on a flat surface and center the design motif on the hoop right side up. Slip the smaller ring into place, securing the fabric in the hoop. Tighten the adjustment screw while pulling the fabric around the edges evenly until it is taut like a drum.

B2 Set the hoop in the machine and stitch the motif. If you need to move the fabric to create the design, move it back and forth or from side to side – don't rotate it, as this will distort the stitch. If your sewing machine comes with its own special embroidery hoop, this may clip into a carriage on the machine so that it will move automatically as required in conjunction with the needle to create the design.

FREE-MOTION MACHINE EMBROIDERY

If you want to create random embroidery patterns or quilting designs – either pre-programed or freehand – you will need to drop the feed dog to work free-motion embroidery. This allows you to move the fabric around under the needle at will, but it requires a bit of practice to get the stitching consistently even. Replace the presser foot with the one recommended in your machine manual for free-motion embroidery or quilting. Lower or cover the feed dog (see page 31) and set the machine stitch length and width controls. Place the fabric, in a hoop if you prefer, under the needle and lower the presser foot so that the thread

tension is active. Using the hand wheel, insert the needle into the fabric and take three or four small stitches to lock the threads in place. Clip off the loose thread ends. Begin stitching the design, moving the fabric or hoop slowly and at an even speed.

Free-motion machine embroidery without a presser foot

You might want to try working without a presser foot if, for example, you are working a really random design in a hoop and the presser foot would get in the way. Hold the fabric tightly against the needle plate or it will pop up and down and the stitches will not interlock correctly. To keep the fabric tight, place two or three fingers of both hands inside the hoop and press down near the area being stitched, but be careful not to put your fingers under the needle. Remember, you still need to have the presser foot lever down – even without the presser foot attached – or the tension mechanism will not operate.

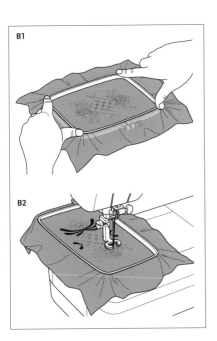

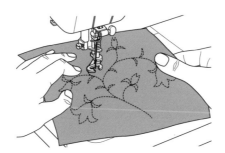

APPLIQUÉ

Appliqué is the traditional technique of applying pieces of fabric or motifs onto a background fabric. It can be used to add extra decorative detail to a small area or to create an entire design, but either way the sewing machine speeds up the process.

SIMPLE MOTIFS

For a simple, single motif, the following method works well.

A1 Place your chosen motif on the right side of the fabric and draw around it. Cut it out with a pair of sharp scissors.

A2 Spray a light coating of temporary spray adhesive over the wrong side of the motif. Place the motif on the background fabric and smooth it into place. The spray adhesive will allow you to adjust the position if necessary.

A3 Set the sewing machine to zigzag stitch with a medium stitch width and a very short stitch length. Stitch carefully around the outline of the appliqué piece.

TIP For best results you will need a good zigzag stitch that can be worked very closely like satin stitch. Many machines also have other decorative stitches that can be used for appliqué.

TIP When working on the wrong side of the fabric, the motif will be reversed when it is right side up. For symmetrical shapes this will not present a problem, but you will need to take this into account if you are using letters or numbers in your design.

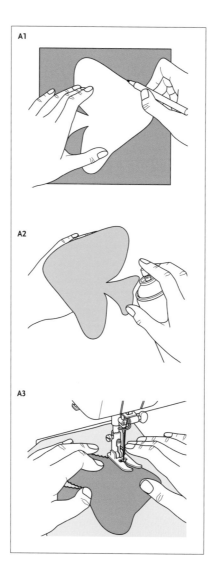

COMPLICATED MOTIFS

When working on more complicated appliqué designs, you can use fusible webbing to attach the appliqué motifs to the background fabric prior to stitching.

B1 First, trace the appliqué motifs required onto the paper backing of pieces of fusible webbing. Use a different piece of fusible webbing for all the appliqué motifs to be cut from each of your chosen fabrics, and lay the shapes close together to save on materials.

B2 Iron the marked-up pieces of fusible webbing onto the reverse side of the selected fabrics. Cut out each motif, leaving the backing paper in place for the moment.

B3 Either mark the center position of the appliqué design on the background fabric with pins, or place the fabric on a light box with the pattern underneath to act as a guide. Peel the backing paper off the appliqué motifs and carefully place the first pieces. Iron them into place.

B4 Add the remaining pieces in order and iron to fix in place. Set the sewing machine to zigzag stitch with a medium stitch width and a very short stitch length, and use the embroidery foot. Machine stitch around the edges of the appliqué pieces. To avoid bulky lines showing through, do not sew along any edges that will be covered by another piece.

B1

B2

B3

B4

PATCHWORK

Patchwork, or piecing, is the art of making larger pieces of fabric by stitching together small pieces. The small pieces can create an overall pattern, or be made into repeating units called blocks, which are joined together. A traditional block quilt is made from repeats of the same block design or several different ones.

STRIPS

A straight seam and an accurate seam allowance are both essential if you want to achieve perfectly aligned strips.

A1 A special foot that measures an exact ¼in (6mm) seam allowance is available for most machines (page 29), but marking the needle plate with a strip of masking tape is just as effective (see Using the Seam Allowance Guide, page 50). Check the measurement on a scrap piece of fabric before you begin sewing a new project and replace the tape when it is worn or grubby.

A2 Cut a good selection of strips in your selected fabrics. Take two and place them right sides together, lining up the raw edges. Stitch the two pieces together, taking care to keep the seam exactly straight and ¼in (6mm) away from the raw edges (see Guiding the Fabric Through the Machine, page 50).

CHAIN PIECING

Chain piecing allows you to stitch many units in sequence without lifting the presser foot or stopping. This example is for four-patch blocks.

B1 Cut a good selection of each of the fabric squares to be used and place in sorted piles near your machine. Join two pieces together to form a unit and feed one unit after another through the machine, stitching continuously without pausing. You will end up with a long chain of 2-piece units, held together by short lengths of thread between each.

B2 Separate the 2-piece units and press open. Take two 2-piece units and place right sides together so the color squares alternate, making a 4-piece unit. Pair all the 2-piece units in this way. Feed all the 4-piece units through the machine as in B1. Cut the threads to separate as before, and press open lightly.

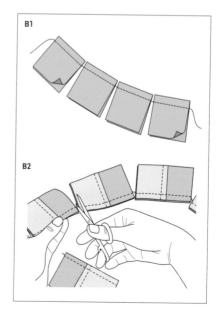

B1

B2

JOINING PIECED UNITS

The biggest problem when joining many pieced units together is getting the seams to line up. Make sure you join pieces together in the correct order, and keep checking the alignment as you work.

C1 Make up a selection of pieced units and press the seams to one side. Place two units right sides together, aligning raw edges and matching seams. Stitch together.

C2 Press the seams to one side on the wrong side (top). On the right side (bottom) the seamlines between the pieces should run in a straight line, with perfectly square corners.

> **TIP** Accurate measuring and stitching is essential at all stages of making a pieced unit. Even a tiny error will be magnified if repeated over several units.

JOINING PLAIN AND PIECED UNITS

Some block designs will call for pieced and plain units to be stitched together in various combinations.

D1 Make up the pieced unit and then cut the plain unit to the same size. This is much easier than trying to make up the pieced unit to match the size of the plain one.

D2 Place the pieced unit and the plain unit right sides together, stitch and press. On the right side the diagonal seam on the pieced unit should fall exactly ¼in (6mm) below the edge of the block.

D3 When the paired units are stitched to the next pair, all the corners should meet exactly in the center.

TRIANGLE SQUARES

Triangle squares are the basis for several traditional block designs. Piecing together two triangles to make a perfect square may sound complex, but it's very easy with this technique.

E1 For each block, cut one square each of fabrics A and B, and two squares of fabric C. Mark a diagonal line on the wrong side of each square, being careful not to stretch the fabric out of shape as you draw on the bias.

E2 With right sides together, place a square of A on top of one square of C and a square of B on top of the other square of C, matching the diagonal lines. Stitch ¼in (6mm) away from the line down one side, then turn and come back ¼in (6mm) away down the other side. Cut along the diagonal line between the two lines of stitching, then press the triangle squares flat with the seams to one side.

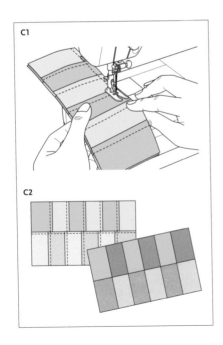

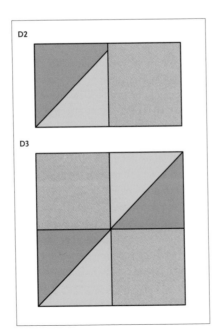

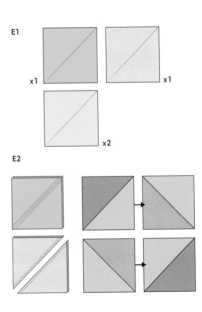

FOUNDATION PIECING

In this technique, pieces are stitched in order onto a foundation, or base, fabric. It is ideal for irregular shapes and edges cut on the bias as the foundation fabric will stabilize them.

F1 Draw the pattern of the block onto the foundation fabric, which can be a non-woven stabilizer or a suitable fabric such as muslin (calico). Number the shapes in the order that they have to be stitched, working from the center outwards.

F2 Trace the pattern of the block onto tracing paper. Cut this into individual pieces and use as templates to cut the fabric pieces, adding a ¼in (6mm) seam allowance all around the edge of each.

F3 Place the foundation fabric onto the work surface, with the unmarked side facing up. Place the first piece of fabric on top in its relevant position and pin in place. Check on the reverse to make sure the fabric piece covers the stitching line all round.

F4 Place the second piece of fabric on top of the first piece, right sides together and with edges aligned so that when it flips over it will be in its correct position in the design. Pin in place.

F5 Working with the marked side of the foundation fabric facing you, stitch the marked line between the first two shapes. Turn over, flip the second piece of fabric into its correct position and press.

F6 Place the third piece of fabric on top of the other two, right sides together and with edges aligned so that when it flips over it will be in its correct position in the design. Pin in place, then sew as before.

F7 Continue to sew on the pieces, keeping to the marked order.

F8 When the block is complete, press and trim to square it up as necessary.

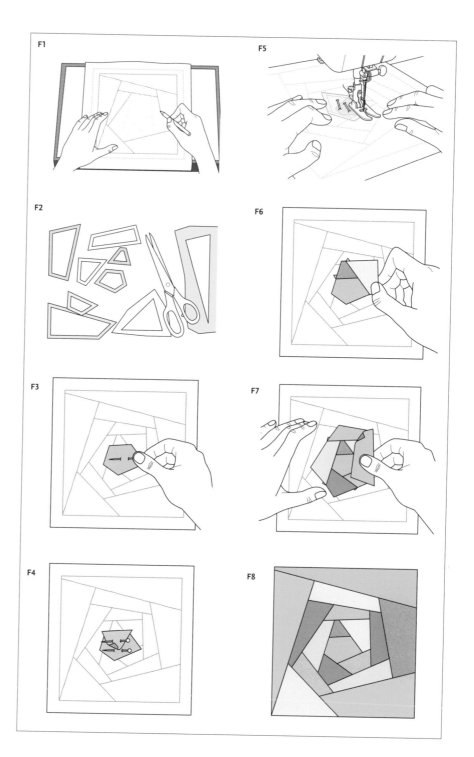

JOINING BLOCKS

After individual blocks have been made and pressed, they need to be joined or set together. There are various standard ways to do this, but an almost endless variety of designs can be created. First, lay all the blocks out on a flat surface and stand back to judge that you are happy with the overall effect.

When joining blocks directly to each other, start by joining all the blocks into strips – you can either work in columns down the quilt, or in rows across. Then join the strips up to make the finished quilt. This is a much more efficient way of working than adding one block at a time to an increasingly large and unwieldy quilt.

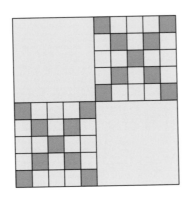

Spacer blocks
Very complex blocks are often spaced out in the design by using plainer blocks between them. These spacer blocks are ideal for machine quilting designs because the stitching lines will show much better on a plain background.

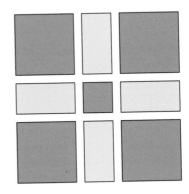

Sashing strips
Alternatively, the blocks can be separated by strips of fabric called sashing, which are often in a contrasting or coordinating color and can be used as a unifying element to bring lots of random blocks into a cohesive design.

Squaring up blocks
Blocks intended for the same quilt may have been worked on over time, or may have been collected from different sources, so they may not be identical. Before joining blocks together, check that they are all the same size and have the same ¼in (6mm) seam allowance. Make sure all the corners are square and that the sides are straight, trimming if necessary.

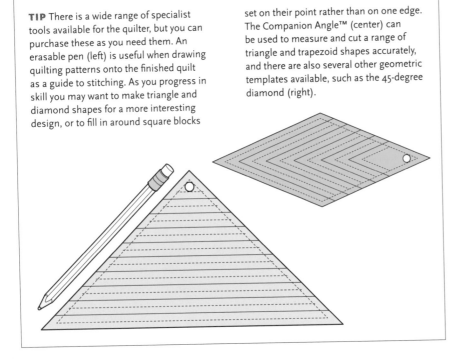

TIP There is a wide range of specialist tools available for the quilter, but you can purchase these as you need them. An erasable pen (left) is useful when drawing quilting patterns onto the finished quilt as a guide to stitching. As you progress in skill you may want to make triangle and diamond shapes for a more interesting design, or to fill in around square blocks set on their point rather than on one edge. The Companion Angle™ (center) can be used to measure and cut a range of triangle and trapezoid shapes accurately, and there are also several other geometric templates available, such as the 45-degree diamond (right).

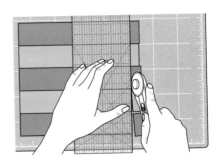

QUILT-AS-YOU-GO

This is a technique in which the blocks have batting added as they are stitched, so after they are joined together the final quilt just needs backing and binding. The technique can also be used to make a small quilt.

G1 Cut the batting approximately 2in (5cm) larger all around than the size of the finished block. Cut all the fabric strips needed to complete the block. Take the first two strips of fabric and place them right sides together, with edges matching. Align the left-hand edge of the strips with the left-hand edge of the batting. Stitch ¼in (6mm) from the right-hand edge of the strips through all three layers. Fold over the top strip so it is right side up.

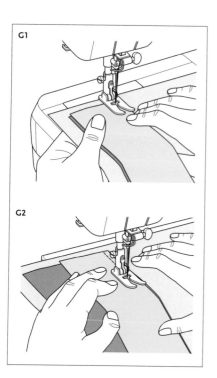

G2 Take the third strip of fabric and place it right sides together on top of the second strip, aligning the right-hand raw edge. Stitch ¼in (6mm) from the right-hand edge of the second and third strips, through all three layers. Fold over the third strip so it is right side up.

G3 Carry on working across the piece of batting in this way, until it is completely covered with fabric. Trim the finished block to square up the edges all around as required.

ASSEMBLING A QUILT

A quilt consists of three layers: the top, which is decorative, the batting in the center that provides warmth, and the backing, which can be plain or can also be decorative to make the quilt reversible. Before the quilt is assembled, the top must be completed by stitching any individual blocks together as described opposite, either directly or using spacer blocks or sashing. Most traditional quilt tops also have a border around all four sides.

If the blocks have been made using the quilt-as-you-go technique, after they have been joined into a top you only need to back the quilt with a piece of fabric cut to the same size and then bind the raw edges on all four sides as described on pages 116–117. If the quilt top has been made using any other technique, you will need to add batting as well as backing. Lay the quilt top right side down and lay the batting on top. Place the backing right side up on top of that and smooth everything flat. Baste the layers in place, working from the center outwards to each corner, then to the middle of each side. The quilt can

then be machine quilted as described on pages 132–133, and finally the raw edges are trimmed level and bound, using the binding technique described on pages 116–117.

BAGGING

With this alternative technique for assembling a quilt, the batting is cut to size and laid out flat, and the quilt top is placed right side up on top of it. The backing is then placed on top of this, right side down. The three layers of the quilt are machine stitched together around the outside edge, leaving a gap in the final side of about a quarter of its length. The quilt is then turned right side out through the gap, which is finally slipstitched closed. There is no need for binding because the edges are finished, so the quilt just needs to be machine quilted to finish it off.

MAKING A QUILT

✄ Before you begin to join patchwork blocks into a quilt, lay them all out on a flat surface and stand back to check you are happy with the overall effect.

✄ When planning your quilt, be aware of how it will be viewed when finished. If it is to be displayed on a bed, you may need to orientate the blocks in different directions at each side so they will be viewed the correct way up when the quilt is in use.

✄ Choose a backing fabric that coordinates with one of the elements in your quilt. It is better to choose a fabric that is the same composition as that used for the quilt top.

MACHINE QUILTING

Quilting is the stitching, usually decorative, that holds the layers of a quilt together. Machine quilting appeared with the advent of the sewing machine, and in the last few years sewing machines specially-designed for quilting have been developed.

QUILTING ON A SEWING MACHINE

You can quilt a lightweight quilt on a good general sewing machine as long as it is heavy-duty enough to stitch through all the layers. If you quilt in-the-ditch – following the lines of the seams that join the parts of the quilt together – you can stitch a slightly heavier weight quilt on a good normal machine too, but for complex quilting designs or full-weight quilts you will be better off with a machine designed for quiltmakers. This is because it will have features such as adjustable foot pressure, a speed limiter and an extension table to give you a good-size sewing bed (see page 20). Well-worked machine quilting can be every bit as attractive as a piece of hand work – and can be completed much quicker.

QUILTING LINES

There are several different methods of quilting (see opposite), but all start from the quilted line, so practice working straight, curved or meandering stitch lines before you begin. Machine quilting is the best option for any quilt that will be laundered frequently.

> **TIP** A domestic sewing machine will generally not have a large sewing area to support a full quilt, so to make it more manageable as you sew, roll up the edges around the area you are working on and secure the rolls with quilt clips. A good substitute for these are bicycle clips.

Straight lines

If you are working in straight lines, either mark the full design on the quilt top or mark the first line and then use the foot as a guide to space the following lines an equal distance away. If the lines are spaced more widely apart, use the special presser foot as described in Curved Lines (above right) to measure the distance.

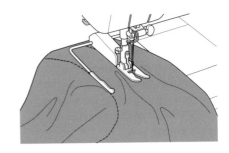

Curved lines

Concentric curved lines can also be marked, or you can use a special presser foot with an extended bar that allows you to follow the line of the previous row of stitching an exact distance away for the next and each following line. Curved lines in a motif must be marked on the fabric in some way before stitching (see Marking Tools, page 67).

Meander stitch

Meander or free-motion quilting is a machine-stitching technique that can be used to add texture to the background, rather than to add a clear quilting design. Drop or cover the feed dog (see page 16) so the quilt can be moved around under the needle in a random way. Ideally, lines of stitching should not cross, so work on small areas at a time and try to plan the general layout of the stitching before you begin.

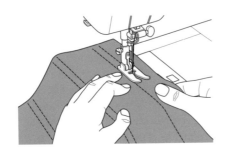

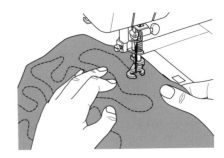

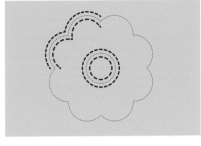

WORKING ON A LARGE QUILT

✂ If you start quilting at one edge, you will have the whole area of the quilt lying to one side and pulling as you work, which will make it hard to maneuver.

✂ Start at the middle and work outwards. This ensures that any fabric take-up caused by the stitching will be distributed much more evenly.

✂ A small table or ironing board placed next to your machine table will help to support a large quilt.

QUILTING METHODS

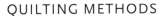

There are several different ways of machine quilting a piece of work. Choose whichever method or methods suit your design best.

In-the-ditch

For discreet quilting, stitch within the seamlines of a pieced pattern, or work exactly around the outline of an appliqué piece. There is no need to mark the quilting pattern since you work along stitching that already exists.

Outline

This is similar to in-the-ditch, but the stitching is positioned around ¼in (6mm) away from the seamline, appliqué edge or motif. It can be worked inside or outside the lines (or even both ways) and there is often no need to mark a pattern.

Echo

With this method, you stitch around the outline of an appliqué piece or motif as above, then keep repeating the outline shape in lines of stitching at close parallel intervals to fill the entire background. Marking will keep the lines and spacing even, or use a quilting bar (see opposite page).

Motif

Marking is essential for this technique. Each individual motif is marked onto the fabric in outline, and then you simply quilt along the lines. The marking lines are usually hidden under the stitching, but just to be safe it is best to use an erasable method.

Filling grids or patterns

With this technique, an all-over grid or pattern is used to fill the background with texture. The stitching can be used to create a secondary design that is not related to the piecing or appliqué design of the quilt top. As with motif quilting, marking is essential, but use an erasable method.

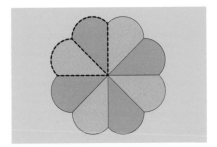

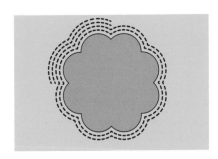

GLOSSARY

appliqué – a piecing process using small amounts of fabric or fabric motifs sewn onto a background fabric in a decorative design. Appliqué can be done by hand, by machine, or with fusible web. Appliqué is a great technique to cover stains, rips or other problem areas on a larger fabric area.

auto-thread function – threads the sewing machine needle automatically.

backing – the bottom or back layer of an item, usually in a plainer fabric than the main material.

backstitch – backstitching on a sewing machine is stitching in reverse for a short distance at the beginning and end of a seam to stop the stitching unraveling. Backstitch is also a hand stitch that creates a row of stitches set end-to-end, looking from the right side like machine stitching, but with the end of each stitch overlapping the next on the wrong side. It is used for mending and to hand-stitch short seams securely.

bagging – a method of backing a fabric item that involves sewing the back and the front, right sides together, around three edges, but leaving a gap in the fourth side. The item is turned right side out through the gap, which is then stitched closed.

bar tack – several short stitches worked parallel and very close together to reinforce the end of an opening, such as at the ends of a buttonhole.

basting – long stitches used to hold layers of fabric together until they are permanently machine stitched. Basting stitches are removed when the stitching is completed. Basting can be done by hand, or by machine using the longest stitch setting.

batting – the filling that forms the central layer of a quilted item.

bias – the diagonal direction across woven fabric at a 45-degree angle to the warp and the weft. Fabric cut on the bias stretches and must be handled with great care. Bias tape allows binding to be carried out around curved edges without pleating.

bias tape or strip – a long, thin length of fabric cut on the bias and used for binding.

binding – a strip of fabric sewn over raw edges to finish and/or decorate the edge. Normally a binding is sewn onto one side, then brought over the edges to the other side, and slipstitched in place. Binding can be straight or cut on the bias.

blind hem – a method of machine hemming using zigzag stitch so that only the very point of the zigzag catches the front piece of fabric, and the stitching hardly shows on the right side.

blocks – a repeating unit made in fabric that is joined together to make a quilt top. The block can be plain, pieced together from smaller pieces of fabric, or decorated with an appliqué or embroidered design.

bobbin – a small spool for holding thread. Sewing machines use two threads to make a stitch – the needle thread, coming downwards from the top of the machine, and the bobbin thread coming upwards from under the needle plate. Bobbins can be top-loading (dropped into the bobbin case through a sliding or hinged panel in the needle plate), or side/front-loading (the bobbin is placed into the bobbin case outside the machine, the filled bobbin case is then inserted into the machine at the front or side through an opening door).

bobbin case – the metal case with tension plates on the side, which holds the bobbin. On top-loading machines, the bobbin case is normally left in place unless it is removed for cleaning, or to change it for a spare or special bobbin case so the bobbin tension can be adjusted for free-motion work. On side/front-loading machines the bobbin case is taken out of the machine before the bobbin can be removed from it.

bodkin – a short, blunt-ended needle that can be used to tease out sharp points and corners in fabric, and to thread thin elastic.

bolt – a length of fabric wound onto a round tube or a flattened oval cardboard form. Wider fabric is usually folded lengthwise, right sides together, before being wound onto the bolt. Wholesale fabric stores sell fabric by the bolt or by the cut length – the amount in a bolt can vary according to the manufacturer and the type of fabric.

border – a strip of fabric, usually in a contrasting or complementary color, sewn to the outer edges of an item to serve as a frame for the interior or to enhance the design.

bound buttonhole – a slit in fabric with bound edges, that fastens over a button.

box pleats – pairs of pleats with each pair pointing towards each other to create a flat, tailored look.

braid – a decorative woven strip used to trim fabric items or to conceal tacks in upholstery.

chain piecing or sewing – a quiltmaking technique in which prepared fabric pieces are fed into the sewing machine continuously, one after the other, without lifting the foot or breaking the thread. This allows many repetitive units to be sewn without stopping after each one, saving on both time and thread.

chain stitch – a type of sewing machine stitch that can be formed of one or two threads. With a single thread, the needle thread passes through to the reverse of the fabric where it loops through itself. If the machine uses two threads, a looper moves back and forth on the reverse of the fabric to create loops in the second thread that the needle thread crosses through. Most modern sewing machines form lockstitch instead of chain stitch.

cone – thread can come wound into a cone-shape on a long spool. A cone contains far more thread than an ordinary spool of thread and cones are often used on embroidery machines and

sergers because both get through large amounts of thread quickly.

continuous binding – binding that runs round four sides in a single length, with miters at the corners ,and only one join at the start/end of the strip of fabric.

cording – also known as corded piping, is piping with a cord inside the fold so it has a more rounded appearance. It is inserted into a seam for decoration.

coverstitch – a serger stitch created with two or three needle threads and one looper thread, and the cutting blades disengaged, to create a hem for stretchy fabrics.

crosswise grain – also known as the cross-grain, weft or width. The crosswise grain of a woven fabric is at right angles to the selvages and has more stretch than the lengthwise threads.

dart – a triangular, stitched tuck running horizontally or vertically in from the edge to shape a flat piece of fabric around the curves of the body. A double-pointed dart runs vertically down the fabric piece, going from a point, widening out, and then back into a point again.

differential feed – a type of fabric feed often found on a serger, with two independent sets of feed dog, one before and one after the needle. By changing their relative motions, these feed dog sets can be used to stretch or compress the material near the needle. This is very useful when you are sewing stretchy material, or for creating special effects.

directional print – fabric with a printed pattern that has a definite direction or grain. Care must be taken to match the direction when joining different lengths. *See also* **nap**.

double binding – binding an edge with a double thickness strip of fabric.

double chain stitch – a serger stitch created with one needle thread and one looper thread, and used for seams or for decorative stitching. It is not flexible enough, however, to use on stretchy fabrics.

double hem – a hem in which the fabric is folded under to the wrong side twice so the raw edge is completely enclosed. The hem is stitched in place along the upper foldline.

drop feed – a term used to describe the process by which the fabric is normally fed through the sewing machine. When the needle moves upwards and withdraws from the fabric, the feed dog comes up through slots in the needle plate, and the serrated top surface grips the material, which is held firmly against it by the presser foot. The feed dog moves horizontally backwards so the fabric is dragged backwards into position for the next stitch. The feed dog is then lowered again, and returns to its original position, while the needle makes its next pass through the material. While the needle is in the material, there is no feed action.

dual feed – an enhancement to drop feed on a sewing machine in which a moving upper foot (separate from the presser foot) clamps the fabric against the feed dog and moves in sync with it to move the fabric, creating an effect similar to a walking foot. It also covers some of the functions of the differential feed on a serger.

ease – to make two edges of different lengths fit together in the same seam. One piece may have to be stretched a little, or bunched up slightly, so that the edges are adjusted to the same length.

easestitching – machine stitching used to very slightly gather the length of an edge to reduce it so it can be joined to a slightly shorter edge without visible folds.

echo quilting – several lines of quilting stitches following the edge of a shape or block, thus echoing the shape.

edgestitching – a line of stitching made close to a seamline, foldline or a finished edge. It is not necessarily decorative, but intended to keep the line crisp.

electronic speed limiter – a function that allows you to set the maximum speed that the machine will stitch with the foot control fully depressed.

embroidery digitizing – the action of converting a graphic design into computerized instructions that tell an embroidery machine how to sew a design.

embroidery hoop – a pair of wooden or plastic circles that clip together, one inside the other, to hold a section of fabric taut for embroidery.

eyelet buttonhole – a completely circular buttonhole that can be used for military-style buttons, for decoration, or to create belt holes.

extension table – this fits onto the machine at the needle end and gives a much larger sewing bed to support large pieces of sewing, such as quilts or home decorating projects.

fabric casing – a tube of fabric through which elastic or cording can be threaded.

faced hem – a hem with a separate strip of fabric stitched on the hemline, right sides together, and then turned to the inside along the hemline. The raw edge of the facing is either turned under and hemmed, or zigzag stitched and machine stitched into place.

facing – a shaped piece of fabric stitched on the seamline, right sides together, and then turned to the inside to create a finished edge.

feed dog – the serrated teeth below the needle plate that grip and move the fabric through the machine. If the feed dog is dropped, the fabric can be moved freely under the needle for free-motion quilting, machine embroidery, or for sewing on buttons.

finger pressing – using your fingers, instead of an iron, to press a seam or fold into fabric.

finished size – the final sewn size of a completed item.

flat bed – a flat bed machine has a base that sits flat on the work surface for its

full length. This may make it hard to stitch narrow cylindrical items, such as sleeves and pant legs. The alternative to a flat bed is a free-arm.

flat-fell seam – a seam designed to give a strong join on heavy-duty fabric subject to wear, and traditionally used on jeans. The seam is stitched wrong sides together. One seam allowance is trimmed back; the other has the edge folded under, and is then pressed flat to cover the trimmed seam allowance. The upper seam allowance is stitched in place along the foldline, giving a double line of stitching on the right side of the fabric, and a join line with a parallel line of stitching on the reverse.

flatlock stitch – a serger stitch created with one needle thread and two looper threads, used for butted or lapped seams and decorative stitching.

foldline – a line marked in fabric by folding over and pressing along the fold.

foot pressure – the weight applied to the fabric by the presser foot when it is in the down position. A machine with adjustable foot pressure will allow you to reduce the pressure when sewing very thin fabrics, or increase it when stitching through many layers.

foundation piecing – a method of assembling a quilt block by sewing pieces to a foundation, or base, of plain fabric. Sewing fabric pieces on a foundation of paper is known as foundation paper piecing.

free-arm – a free-arm sewing machine has the base cut away underneath at the needle plate end, to give an 'arm' raised above the work surface. Narrow cylindrical items, such as sleeves and pant legs, can be threaded onto the arm for easier stitching. The free-arm is often brought into use by detaching a piece on the base of the machine, leaving the arm protruding. The alternative to a free-arm is a flat bed.

free-motion quilting – a type of machine quilting in which the feed dog is lowered or covered so the quilter can create the design by moving the quilt sandwich under the needle at will.

French seam – a seam in which the fabric is stitched with wrong sides together first, then folded back along the seamline, and stitched again right sides together so the raw edges are fully enclosed. It is ideal for sheer fabrics, where the raw edges of a normal seam would be visible on the right side. *See also* **mock French seam**.

frill – a length of fabric gathered along one long edge and stitched to a flat piece. Also known as a ruffle.

fringe trim – trimming with long, even loops or threads hanging off one edge.

fusible interfacing – *see* **interfacing**.

fusible web – an adhesive web that can be ironed onto a fabric to adhere two layers of fabric, for easier appliqué for example, or for hemming.

gather – reducing the length of a piece of fabric by stitching down one edge, then pulling the fabric up along the stitching thread into unstructured pleats.

grading seams – trimming the seam allowances down to different widths after a seam is stitched, to eliminate bulk.

grain – the direction of the lengthwise (warp) and crosswise (weft) threads of a fabric. The lengthwise grain, parallel to the selvage, stretches least and should be used for borders whenever possible. The crosswise grain, at right angles to the selvage, has slightly more give.

hand wheel – a wheel on the right-hand end of a sewing machine or serger that can be turned by hand to raise or lower the needle. On some models the hand wheel can only be turned in one direction.

hem – a method of neatening a raw edge by turning the edge under once or twice and stitching in place.

hem allowance – the width of fabric from the hemline that will be turned up to create a hem.

hemline – the bottom edge of the hem.

hemming stitch – a hand stitch used to secure a hem so only small inconspicuous stitches show on the right side.

hook and bar – a type of fastening with a metal hook and a corresponding bar. The hook and the bar are stitched on opposite sides of an opening. Sometimes the hook is paired with a circular eye instead of the bar, in which case the fastening is called a hook and eye.

hook cover plate – on a top-loading machine, this is a removable section in the needle plate that covers the bobbin in its casing.

hook race – the circular route around the bobbin that the hook travels to loop the needle thread around the bobbin thread.

in-seam buttonhole – the simplest type of buttonhole, a gap within the length of a seam.

in-the-ditch quilting – quilt stitching within the seamlines of a pieced pattern. Also known as ditch quilting.

interfacing – a compressed synthetic fabric used as a backing to the main project fabric, particularly in dressmaking and tailoring, to give extra body, shaping and support. An interfacing can either be sew-in or fusible.

invisible stitching – sewing that does not show on the right side of the item, usually achieved by taking a very tiny stitch from the back, through only a single thread of the fabric.

knee lifter – a long lever that extends down at the front of the machine so that it can be pushed with one knee, enabling the presser foot to be lifted and the feed dog dropped without letting go of the fabric being stitched. It is not available on all machines, but is useful for quilting, sewing around intricate shapes, and appliqué.

knife pleats – a series of single pleats made to the same width, and all pointing in the same direction.

lapped seam – a type of seam in which the edges are overlapped and stitched, and used to join pieces with minimum bulk. Ideal for interfacing, interlining, and thick fabrics that do not fray.

LCD screen – a Liquid Crystal Display screen is the thin, flat panel used for electronically displaying information on an electronic sewing machine.

lettuce edge – an edge finish in which the fabric edge is stretched as it is overcast, creating a ruffled effect. It is usually created on a serger by using the differential feed function.

light box – a box with a translucent plastic top and lighting inside.

lint – the dust and tiny pieces shed from thread and fabric while sewing, which builds up as fluff around the hook race, bobbin casing and feed dog mechanism. It should be cleaned away regularly.

lockstitch – the stitch performed by most modern sewing machines. One thread comes down through the needle, and a second thread comes up from the bobbin. The needle takes a loop of thread through the fabric and down through the hole in the needle plate, where it is caught by a rotary hook and looped around the thread from the bobbin. The needle thread and bobbin thread each stay on their own side of the fabric, but interlock in the middle, creating a stitch that looks the same on both sides.

looper – a serger uses one or more loopers instead of a bobbin. The looper threads lock around each other and are linked together with the needle thread to form the stitches.

meander quilting/stitching – a free-motion machine quilting technique that can be used to add texture to the background, rather than to add a clear quilting design.

metallic needles – constructed specifically for use with metallic and monofilament threads. They are thin, with a sharp point to eliminate thread breakage, an elongated eye to make threading easier, and an elongated scarf to prevent shredding. Metallic machine embroidery needles are available in sizes 10/70 through 14/90.

mitered corner – a corner (usually of a border) that is joined at a 45-degree angle, like a picture frame.

mock French seam – a seam in which the fabric is stitched right sides together, then the two raw edges of the seam allowance are folded inwards to the seamline and hemmed together along the foldline, to give the look of a French seam. *See also* **French seam**.

mock safety stitch – a serger stitch created with either two needle threads and one looper thread, or two needle threads and two looper threads, and used for seams on stretchy fabrics. *See also* **safety stitch**.

monogram – a design of intertwined initial letters, usually embroidered.

motif – a single design element in a printed pattern on fabric, or a patch used for appliqué.

nap – a soft fabric surface, made by brushing all the short fibers in one direction. Depending on which way the light falls on the fabric, it can look lighter or darker; items would normally be constructed with the nap running in the same direction on each adjacent piece, unless the play of light and dark is being used as a design feature. To achieve the nap running in the same direction often requires more fabric, particularly when dressmaking, as pattern pieces cannot be reversed to fit in with each other when laying them out on the fabric. *See also* **pile**.

needle clamp – the open end of the needle bar that has an adjustable screw, which is turned to hold onto or release the needle.

needle plate – the removable plate that fits over the feed dog and the bobbin, with a hole that the needle passes through. The plate often has a series of lines etched on it to show different distances from the needle and that can be used to stitch accurate seams.

needle-punch felting – a felting technique in which barbed needles are used to punch through the fabric fibers causing them to mesh together.

notions – a general term covering small sewing items used in the construction of projects, such as thread, needles, pins, zippers, buttons, trims and bindings. Also known as sewing notions or haberdashery.

outline quilting – a form of quilting that outlines a pieced or appliqué design. *See also* **echo quilting**.

overcasting – a type of stitching taken over the raw edges being stitched together, so it neatens the edges and prevents them fraying. It can be done on an ordinary sewing machine by using a close set zigzag stitch close to the edge, but a special overcasting foot is normally required to prevent the fabric edge from curling in as it is stitched.

overlock stitch – a serger stitch created with one needle thread and one or two looper threads, and used for finishing edges and for seams.

overlocker – *see* **serger**.

patchwork – an older term for piecing fabric squares together. Often pieced quilts are referred to as patchwork.

pattern repeat – *see* **repeat**.

piecing – a process of sewing pieces of fabric together, by hand or machine, to create a larger piece of cloth. Also referred to as patchwork.

pile – raised threads or loops on the surface of a fabric. Pile fabric often also has a nap. *See also* **nap**.

pin tuck – a very fine, narrow tuck in fabric. Pin tucks are usually worked in groups of three or more.

piping – a strip of flat, folded fabric inserted into a seam for decoration. *See also* **cording**.

pleats – folds in fabric that are usually only held in place at the top, with the length of the pleat pressed in a straight line to the bottom edge.

pouncing – a technique used to transfer markings to fabric in embroidery and tailoring. A pin, dressmaker's wheel or unthreaded sewing machine needle is used to make holes along the lines of the design on paper. The paper is then pinned to the fabric and fine chalk dust, or special pounce powder, is brushed through the holes. The powder can also be dabbed through the pricked holes using a small piece of rolled up felt.

presser foot – the piece of metal or plastic that sits below the needle. It can be lowered to hold the fabric in place against the feed dog so that it doesn't move about as it is stitched. The actual foot section can usually be removed, and there is a range of special presser feet for different tasks.

princess seam – a seam used when an inward (concave) edge must be stitched to an outward (convex) edge.

quilt – an item made from two layers of fabric with a layer of filling, such as batting (wadding), in between. The top layer of fabric is usually decorative and the backing is plainer, but both sides can be decorative to make the quilt reversible.

quilt-as-you-go – a quiltmaking technique in which the blocks have batting (wadding) added as they are stitched, so that after they are joined together, the final quilt only needs backing and binding.

quilting – machine or hand stitching that holds the layers of a quilt together permanently.

repeat – measurement between the centers of identical motifs running in a straight line lengthwise along printed or woven fabric. A half-drop repeat fabric is when the motifs are identical but staggered, so the motifs in one row crosswise fall halfway between the motifs in the rows above and below.

rickrack – a type of flat braid made in a zigzag design.

rolled hem – a very narrow hem made by rolling the edge of the fabric over just until the raw edge is enclosed, then stitching in place. Rolled hems can be hand or machine stitched.

rouleau loop – a narrow tube of fabric with the ends stitched into the seam of an item, so it will loop over a corresponding button.

rows – the lines of stitches that run across the width of a knitted fabric. *See also* **wales**.

ruffle – *see* **frill**.

running stitch – a hand stitch most often used to join flat layers of fabric together.

safety stitch – a serger stitch made using either four or five threads. For a four-thread safety stitch, a double chain stitch is formed with one needle and one looper and an overlock stitch with another needle and looper simultaneously. For the five-thread version an extra looper is used. *See also* **mock safety stitch**.

sashing – strips of plain fabric running the length and width of a quilt top to separate pieced and spacer blocks. Sashing strips can be used to coordinate several very different block designs into one cohesive quilt top, to set off the block design, or to add extra length and width to the top.

scalloped edge – decorative edge finish stitched in a series of small even curves.

seam allowance – the width from the raw edge of the fabric to the stitching line of the seam.

seamline – the line of stitching on a seam; this is generally ⅝in (15mm) from the seam edge.

self-bound seam – a technique in which one edge of the seam allowance is folded over to encase the other edge.

selvage – the outer edges of a length of fabric, which is usually more tightly woven and so is normally cut off and discarded. Manufacturer's information is often given on the selvage.

serger – a type of sewing machine that makes overcast seams and can cut off the excess seam allowance automatically as it stitches. Also known as an overlocker.

sewing bed – the bottom section of the reverse C-shape of a sewing machine, which houses the bobbin and forms a base to work on.

sharps – small, thin sewing needles with really sharp points that pierce the thread of woven fabrics easily. Available in sizes 8/60–14/90, they are a good choice for straight stitch sewing.

shirring elastic – a type of very thin elastic cord that is very stretchy. It is usually stitched to fabric in parallel rows to create an effect rather like traditional smocking.

single binding – binding an edge with a single thickness strip of fabric.

single hem – a hem in which just one layer of fabric is pressed to the wrong side and stitched in place. The raw edge can be neatened with zigzag stitch first.

slipstitch – a hand stitch used to join two folded edges together, or to secure a folded edge to a flat piece of fabric.

spacer block – a plain block used in quilting to set off the design of more complex blocks, or to eke out a limited number of such blocks so there are enough for a full quilt top.

spindle – the pin that holds the bobbin when winding thread onto it.

spool – the reel that holds the thread.

spool holder/cap – a removable plastic disk on some machines that is pushed onto the spool pin over the thread spool, holding this steady so the thread unwinds smoothly during stitching.

spool pins – the pins to take the thread spools or cones.

stabilizer – a firm gauze used to support fabric, particularly when it is being machine-embroidered. A stabilizer can remain in place permanently, but is usually cut-away, tear-away, heat-away or wash-away.

staystitching – a single or double line of straight stitching within the seam allowance through only a single thickness of fabric, made to stabilize stretch fabrics or curved lines to prevent them from stretching.

stencil – a type of template used to mark embroidery or quilting patterns onto fabric. The design is cut out of a piece of plastic or cardboard, and marking is done by drawing through the openings.

stitch selector – on the more basic sewing machines, the stitch selector is often a dial that allows you to select from a small number of different stitch types. On computerized machines selection from a wide range of stitches is made by pressing a key or using a touch pad.

stitch tension – for even and balanced stitching, each of the threads must be at the correct tension relative to each other. The tension on each thread used can be adjusted individually to achieve this. *See also* **tension mechanism**.

straight of grain – straight along the lengthwise (warp) grain of the fabric. *See also* **bias**.

straight stitch – the most basic type of machine stitching with the stitch length set at around 2–3 and the stitch width at 0.

tacking – *see* **basting**.

tailor's tacks – used to transfer symbols from a paper pattern to several layers of fabric at the same time. Using doubled thread, take the needle through both layers of fabric to make a large stitch through the symbol, but leave a large loop of thread on the pattern side rather than pulling the stitch tight. Snip the loop and remove the pattern; then the layers of fabric can be eased apart and the threads snipped between them, leaving a few strands of thread to mark the place in each layer of fabric.

template – a shape used as a pattern for appliqué motifs or sections of a pieced design, or for tracing lines to be embroidered or quilted. Templates can be purchased or cut from cardboard or template plastic.

tension mechanism – the adjustable plates on a sewing machine or serger that the thread must go through to place it under tension so that the stitch can be formed correctly. *See also* **stitch tension**.

thumbscrew – a tiny, flat screw that can usually be turned with the ball of the thumb.

ties – strips of fabric, or lengths of fabric tubing, set on either side of an opening. These are tied in bows to close the opening.

topstitching – an extra line of stitching made parallel to a finished edge, usually done in contrasting thread as a decorative feature.

thread guides – the guides that take the thread from one point to the next along the threading run.

thread take-up lever – a lever with an eye on the front of a machine that moves up and down with the needle and controls the amount of thread needed for stitching.

threading run – the route of the thread from spool to needle or looper.

treadle – a foot pedal that is pressed up and down to power a manual sewing machine via a belt.

triangle squares – squares of fabric, typically used in piecing designs, made up of two right-angle triangles joined together along the diagonal edge.

tuck – a fold in fabric that is stitched in place along its full length.

wadding – *see* **batting**.

wales – the columns of stitches that run the length of a knitted fabric. *See also* **rows**.

warp – the long threads in woven fabric that run from top to bottom in the length of the material, parallel to the selvage. The warp is also sometimes known as the floating yarn/thread.

weft – the shorter threads in woven fabric that run from side to side. The weft is also sometimes known as the filling yarn, the filler or the woof.

welt seam – a strong seam used to create bulk-free seams on heavy materials. The fabric is stitched wrong sides together; the lower seam allowance is trimmed back and the upper seam allowance is pressed flat to cover it, before being stitched in place. For neatness, the raw edge of the upper seam allowance can be finished with an overcast or zigzag stitch before it is stitched down.

zigzag – stitching in which the needle moves from side to side to create a double-pointed line. The stitch width controls the width of the line of zigzag, and the stitch length controls how tightly together the stitches are.

zipper – a linear fastening with plastic, nylon or metal teeth, mounted on a colored tape.

INDEX